LEARN STM32 WITH PROJECT

Programming for Embedded Systems real-time
embedded systems using AT24C08, Software and more

By

Aharen san

TABLE OF CONTENTS

SOFTWARE INSTALLATION

Hi, welcome to the first project. In this project, I will teach you how to install the software that are necessary for this project. So, let's get started. After finishing this project, you will be able to install STM32QPIMX, Kyle MegaVision and ST-Link USB Driver. Before I start with the install license set, I would like to make sure you are aware of what is STM32QPIMX and Kyle MegaVision. STM32QPIMX is a graphical software used for generating C code which is based on HAL library for parallel initialization. This is a really good software especially for beginners in 32-bit microcontrollers. Because compared to 8-bit microcontrollers, the 32-bit microcontrollers have a lot of peripherals that are quite complex to configure manually by reading the register definition in datasheets. The learning curve is quite high, so for beginners in 32-bit microcontrollers, I recommend you to use QPIMX. QPIMX is used only for generating the C code and cannot be used for editing, compiling and debugging the code. So, you need an IDE. Kyle MegaVision is one of the IDE for ARM microcontrollers programming. Actually, this IDE can be used for all ARM microcontrollers not only from ST, such as ArtMail, NXP or other ARM-based microcontrollers.

STM32CubeMX   Keil uVision

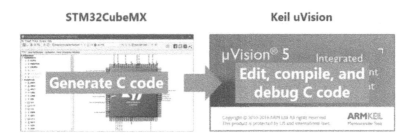

So, I think it is a good investment to learn this IDE because if in the future you need to move to another ARM-based microcontroller, you don't need to learn a new IDE again. Okay, let's move to the software installation. There are 7 files that you need to download. The first one is STM32QPIMX. This is the installer for QPIMX. And then STM32QPF1. This is the HAL library for STM32F1 microcontroller. If you are using another version of STM32, for example STM32F4, then you can search for that. And then this one is the installer for ST-Link USB Downloader.

Name	Date modified	Type	Size
en.stm32cubef1.zip	21 Feb 2017 01:44 ...	WinRAR ZIP archive	79,148 KB
en.stm32cubemx.zip	05 Jul 2017 08:43 A...	WinRAR ZIP archive	298,057 KB
en.stsw-link009.zip	05 Jul 2017 08:20 A...	WinRAR ZIP archive	5,187 KB
jre-8u121-windows-x64.exe		Application	62,650 KB
Keil.STM32F1xx_DFP.2.2.0.p...		uVision Software ...	49,335 KB
MDK523.EXE	05 Jul 2017 08:33 A...	Application	737,407 KB
MDKCM523.EXE	05 Jul 2017 08:36 A...	Application	340,828 KB

Type: WinRAR ZIP archive
Size: 291 MB
Date modified: 05 Jul 2017 08:43 AM

)

ɔbile F

To download the QPIMX, you can go to Google and
search for STM32QPIMX. Click this link, then click this
button to download the software. You must enter your
name and then your email address. After that, the link
for downloading the software will be sent to your
email.

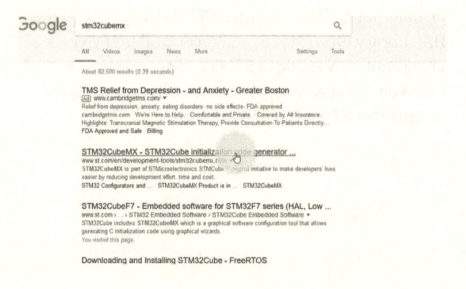

To download the HAL library, you can search for STM32QPIMX. If you are using F1, then click this. And then you can click this button. To download the ST-Link USB Driver, you can search for ST-Link Driver. Click this link to download the USB Driver. And then you can click this button. And then after that, you need to download Java. Java is needed in order to install the QPIMX.

To download Java, you can search for GRE. And then click this link, accept the license agreement, and then you can download the installer depending on your operating system. These three files.

This is the installer for the KL Microvision IDE. This is the legacy support. And this is the software packs. If you are using another version of STM32, then you can search for another version instead of F1. To download KL, you can go to Google and search for KL MDK. Click this link. And click this button to download the MDK Lite version. The MDK Lite version has only a code limitation of 32KB, but it is enough for all of the projects in this project. Click this button to download the MDK code. To download the legacy support, you can click this link. And then click this button.

To download the MDK software packs, you can search for KL MDK software packs. Click this link. You can search for your microcontroller, which is STMicroelectronics. If you are using F1, then you can download F1. And click this button. After all of this file downloaded, you can begin the installation. You can begin the installation with the Java runtime environment. After that, you can install the KubeMX and then the ST-Link USB driver. After that, you can continue to the KL MDK and then you can install the KL legacy support. Here are tips for you when installing KL microvision.

 I recommend you to install KL in a folder that not has a space in each name, for example, C backslash KL version 5.

This PC > Windows 10 (C:)

Name	Date modified	Type
eSupport	04 Mar 2017 02:58 ...	File folder
Intel	19 Jun 2017 07:14 ...	File folder
PerfLogs	16 Jul 2016 06:47 P...	File folder
Program Files	07 Jul 2017 03:44 P...	File folder
Program Files (x86)	05 Jul 2017 09:23 A....	File folder
ProgramFiles	07 Jul 2017 03:29 P...	File folder
ProgramPortable	09:01 A...	File folder
Users	11:02 ...	File folder
Windows	13 Jul 2017 05:48 P...	File folder

Date created: 04 Mar 2017 11:57 PM
Folders: altera

Avoid to install it in a folder that has a space in each name, for example, program space files, because there will be some problem occured if you install KL in this folder. You can install KL in another folder that not has a space, for example, program files without space. Actually, I usually install softwares that cannot be installed in folder that has a space in this folder. This is my KL installation folder. Here I will show you how to install the HAL libraries.

After you install the KubeMX, you can go to Help, install new libraries. Here there is a list of HAL libraries that are available. Here the green button indicates that this library which is for STM32f1 has already installed in my computer.

To install this, you can click this button and then search for the HAL library. Click open. To install the KL software packs, you can click this button and then go to File, Import, and then search for KL software packs. This one. And then click open.

Ok, this is the end of this project. In this project, you have learned how to install the software that are necessary for this project.

NEW PROJECT

Hi, welcome to the project number 2.1. In this project, I will teach you how to make a new project for STM32 by using STM32 cube MX and Kailh Microvision IDE. So, let's get started. After finishing this project, he will be able to create a new project using STM32 cube MX and also build the project and program the STM32 using Kailh Microvision IDE. In this project, I will use this board for most of the project. This board is based on STM32 F1 microcontroller. For some of the project, I will use the STM32 F4 Discovery board which is based on STM32 F4 microcontroller. If you have any STM32 board, you can use this board. You don't have to buy a new board for this project.

The STM32 F1 board that I will use doesn't have an on-board USB downloader.

STM32F1   STM32F4

So, you must have a USB downloader to download the program into the microcontroller. To do that, you can use the ST-Link version 2 USB downloader. You can use either the current version or the original version. If you are using STM32 F4 Discovery, you don't need a USB downloader because this board already has an on-board ST-Link downloader. Here, in this part of the board is a ST-Link USB downloader.

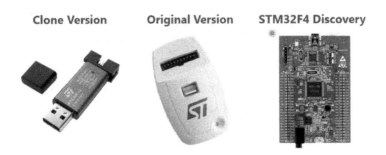

Clone Version **Original Version** **STM32F4 Discovery**

You can even use this ST-Link downloader to program another STM32 by using these pins and remove this jumper.

Okay, in this section, I will show you how to create a new project by using STM32 cubeMX and then I will open that project in the iomicrofusion IDE.

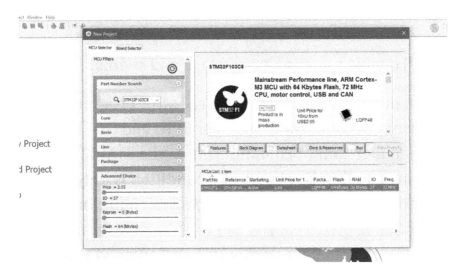

First, you can click new project and then search for your microcontroller. For example, in this case, I use STM32 F103 C8. I will choose this microcontroller and click the stop project button. First of all, you need to enable the system debugger in the peripherals. This peripheral is one of the most important thing for all of your project. You can select the Serial Wire interface for the debugging interface.

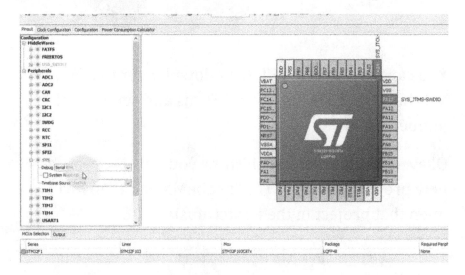

It will enable two pins as sw-clock and sw-dataio.

If you don't enable this peripheral, after programming, these two pins become a normal GPIO and ST-Link downloader cannot communicate to the STM32 microcontroller. However, that condition is only temporary condition, not a permanent condition. If that condition is occurred, you can fix it by reprogramming with the system debugger peripheral enabled. And when you download the code to your STM32, you must press the reset button on your microcontroller board because the ST-Link downloader cannot communicate to the STM32. And after that, you can return back to the normal condition again. The LED in my board is on pin PC13. So, I can click on this pin and enable this pin as GPIO output.

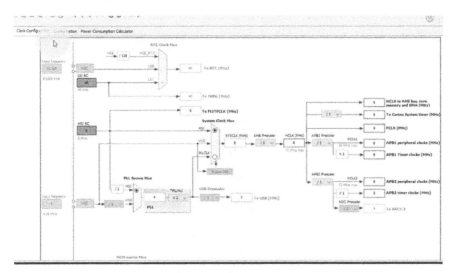

Next, in the clock configuration tab, in this tab, you can configure the system clock. The default setting is 8 MHz. For now, I will not change this setting and I will leave this setting to the default settings. In the configuration tab, you can select the GPIO settings. Here, you can change the GPIO default output level, GPIO mode, and output speed. And also, you can give the user label to your GPIO pin. For example, I name it as

Click ok. Now, you are ready to generate the C code for the Peripherals initialization. Go to the project and click settings. Enter the project name and select your IDE which is KLMDKARM version 5. Go to the code generator tab. In this option, you can select whether you want to copy the library files into your project folder or not. If you choose this first option, then all of the whole library files will be copied into your project folder. Type 4, the size of your project folder will be big. If you select this option, only the necessary whole library files will be copied into your project folder.

If you select this last option, the necessary whole library files will be added as a reference to your project. Type 4, the size of your project folder will be small. In this case, I will choose this last option. In this settings, you can select to enable this option to optimize the power consumption by setting all V pins as analog. Click the ok button and then go to project, click generate code. The code will be generated. Click this button to open the project. The KLMDKARM IDE will be code automatically after you press that button. Here you can open the main.c file.

Here you can see there is a command that indicate where you can place a user code application. For example, user code begin includes, user code end includes. You can place your input between in this command. And also there is a lot of user code section. It is recommended to place your user code between this command. So when you back to STM32QMX and change the settings and then regenerate the user code, will not be deleted. For now, I will add user code application to blinking the LED for every one second. This is the code. After that, you can save this file.

And then you can build the project by pressing this button. This is the result. There is no evolves and warning. After that, you can connect your STLINK downloader to your USB port. And then go to the flash, configure flash tools, select the debug tab. Make sure in this option, the STLINK debugger is selected. And then click the settings button. Make sure the port is SW interface.

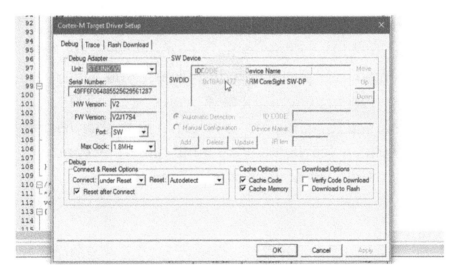

And then in this part, your microcontroller is detected. Go to the flash download tab and enable the reset and run option. If you not enable this option, then after downloading, your program will not run automatically.

Therefore you must reset your STM32 by press the reset button on your STM32 board. Click ok.

Click this button for download the code. This is the result. The LED is blinking for every 1 second. Ok, this is the end of this project. In this project, you have learned how to generate a new project with STM32 QPIMAX and then open the project in Kyle Microvision. You also have learned how to build the project and program the STM32 microcontroller.

SYSTICK TIMER

Hi, welcome to project number two. In this project I will teach you about district timer and how to use this timer for generating a device. So let's get started. After finishing this project, you will be able to bring an aldi with cystic time app using blocking delay and also non blocking delay. This is the simplified block diagram of assistive timer. The assistive time app is located inside the cortex M processor.

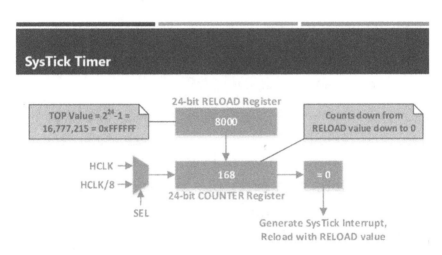

The width of counter register is 24 bits, so the top value is about 16 million. The timer will count on from the reward value one clock cycle. For example, if you set the reward value to 80, then it will count on from 80.

The clock source can be selected either from x clock or x clock divided by eight. When the contact edition is with zero, the system drop will be generated.

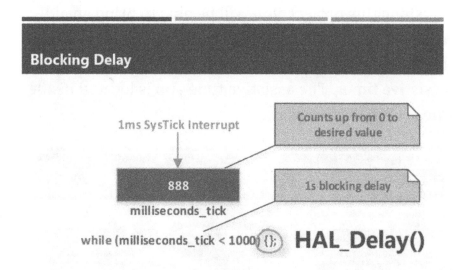

Let's say you have configured your cystic timer to generate an interrupt every one millisecond. Then you have a variable called millisecond stick that will increment it by one FDC stick interrupt which is one Ms. Then you can make a delay by a simple while loop writing for the variables to update the desired failure. For example 1000. If you want to create a 1 second delay inside the loop, they're starting to loop. So the processor just has to wait until the variable reads 1000. This method is called blocking delay because the processor cannot do anything except interrupt surface routine. The hall delay function in Hal algorithm is a blocking UI function. Let me show you a simple code how blocking delay works. In this example, I use two Led one red and one yellow and one switch. The function of this code is to bring the red Led every second. This is the how the line function. The function of the squad is to check the sweet. If the switch is pressed, then the yellow Led will turn on. If we release this width, then the Led will turn off. This is how the program works. The red Led is blinking for 3 seconds as expected. When I press the switch, the yellow Led is not turned on immediately but has to wait for about 3 seconds.

And also when I release the switch, the yellow Led will not turn off immediately but have to wait about 3 seconds. This condition happens because in this line there is a blocking delay. So the processor must wait for 3 seconds before can check the suite in this slide.

Therefore, for the works case, the suite is checkered every 3 seconds. If we want the suite respond immediately after you press it, then you must use another Dy method called nonblocking delay. Here I will show you how to modify the program by using a nonblocking delay. First you have to enable the system debugger in the system.

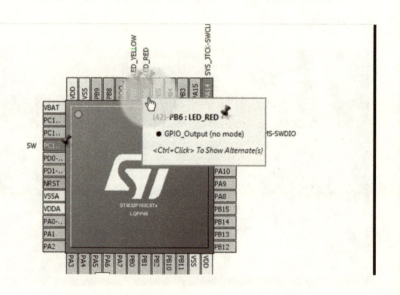

And then you have to set two GPIO as GPI output. For example PB six and PB seven. This one is for red Led and this one is for yellow Led and also for switch. In this case I use PC 15 as a GPIO input in the clock configuration tab you don't have to change anything in the configuration tab. In the GPIO you can activate the pull up SD stuff of the switch and then you have to generate this code. This is the code that has been generated by dupene. In this function there is initialization for CC timer. First I will explain how the generated code for CC timer works. Here the function of this line is to set the result value to equal to the x clock frequency divided by 1000.

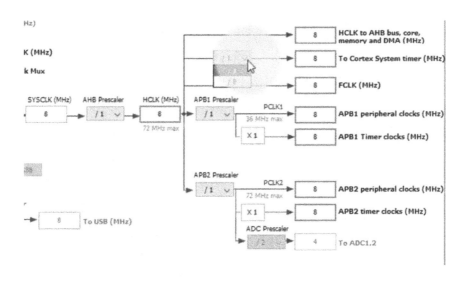

You can see in the clock configuration the s clock is equal to eight MHz so H club divided by 1000 will be equal to 8000. The function of this score is to select the Xcorp as the soft scope for CF timer. This settings correspond to the settings in Qpmx. In Q prime x the system timer is set to 8 MHz which is equal to the 08:00. This is because the press calc is one. You can set the press scalar to eight if you need. And then the function of this code is to enable the cystic interact. Here I will explain a bit about the how the UA function, how the how TheOA function works. You can go to this folder and then open this file f one SSL. This is the Hal library code.

You can see in this line there's a variable called UW tick which is the millisecond stick variable. And then in this line there's a function called how incrementek which will increment it variable. This function itself will be called in the interrupt surface routine. You can see in this file STM 22 f one Fxit. Here. The CDK handle interact. In this inter panel that function is called all incremented. Inside this function there's a while loop that will wait until this value is larger than the delay value. While you are waiting there is nothing to do. So the processor will not do anything except for the interactive Facebook team. This is how delay function works. So it is a blocking delay function.

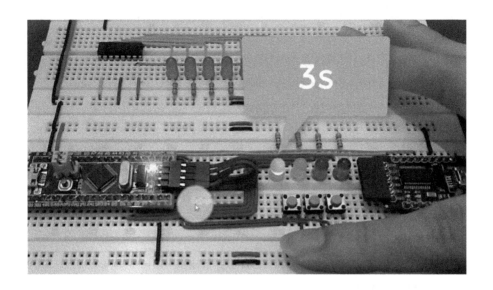

Now I will show you how to make a non blocking delay. Here in the main code I have add a new variable called tickstart which will stop the current tickstart value.

In this line you have to initialize the tickstart variable with the current tick value in the main loop you can check whether the 3 seconds has elapsed or not by this if condition. If three second has elapsed then we have to toggle the red Led by this line of code. And then we have to reinitialize the start of the nest toggling defense.

SYSTEM CLOCKS CONFIGURATION

Hi, welcome to the project number 3.1. In this project, I will teach you about system clocks configuration. So, let's get started. After finishing this project, you will be able to configure the system clocks using external crystal and then set the system clock frequency to the maximum value and also use the KL Microvision Debugger to debug the STM32. Here, I will show you the reference manual of the STM32 microcontroller. This is for STM32 F101, 2, 3, 5 and 7 series. You can download this document from s3.com.

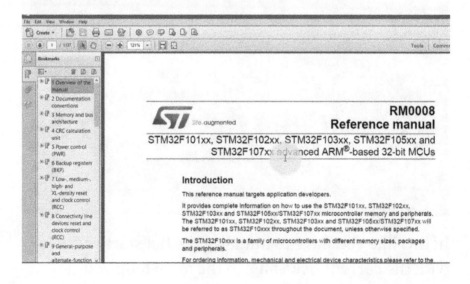

This reference manual contains all of the information about STM32 peripherals.

So, if you want to know more about STM32 peripherals, you can read this document. In this project, I will show you about the clock configuration. So, you can go to chapter 7, go to clocks. Here, you can see the clock tree diagram for this microcontroller.

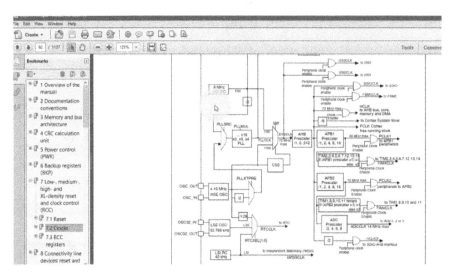

There are two main clock sources that can be used to drive the system clocks. 8 MHz high speed internal RC oscillator and then the 4 to 16 MHz high speed external oscillator. Both the high speed internal or the high speed external can be connected to the system clock directly or through the PLL to multiply the clock value so you can get a more higher clock speed.

There are also two secondary clock sources, the low speed internal RC which is 40 kHz and then low speed external oscillator which is 32 kHz. The LSI can be used to drive the independent wash clock and also the RTC, while the LSE can be used only to drive the RTC. The SISC clock is used to drive the ASB bus, the Cortex-M3 processor core, memory and DMA. And also the Cortex-SISC timer, and then the APB1 peripherals, and then the APB2 peripherals. And there are also other peripheral clocks. Okay, in this demo, I will show you how to configure the system clock using high speed external oscillator and set the frequency to the maximum value.

First, you have to enable the system debug peripheral. And then, if you go to clock configuration tab, here you can see the clock tree diagram like we saw before in the reference manual. By default, the high speed external option is disabled.

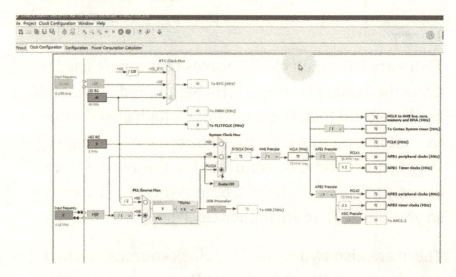

To enable this, you have to enable the external crystal pin in pinout configuration. You can go to pinout, and then select FCC, and then you can enable this pin. These two pins will be used to connect to the crystal oscillator. Here in the clock configuration tab, you can set the external crystal value. In my box, the external crystal value is 8 MHz.

After that, you can set the S-clock frequency to the maximum value, which is 72 MHz. For this microcontroller. And then press enter. The CubeMX will automatically calculate the required PLL value and the prescaler value in order to achieve the 72 MHz clock. The result is high speed external oscillator is selected, and the prescaler is 1. After that, the 8 MHz clock will be multiplied by 9 in order to achieve 17 MHz. The ASB bus clock, core clock, memory, and DMA is 72 MHz. System timer is also 72 MHz. And the clock 1 is 36 MHz, the clock 2 is 72 MHz. In the configuration tab, you don't have to change anything.

And then after that, you can generate the code. Here, in the main.c file, there is a function called System Clock Config. This function is generated by CubeMX to configure the system clock. Let me explain how this function works. There is two structs that will be used to initialize the RCC. One for oscillator and one for the clock. The function of this line is to select the oscillator that you want to initialize, which is the high speed external. And then you have to turn on the high speed external oscillator. And then select the prescaler to 1. These three lines of code correspond to steps 1, 2, and 3 in the clock 3 diagram.

This is for select which oscillator that we want to initialize.

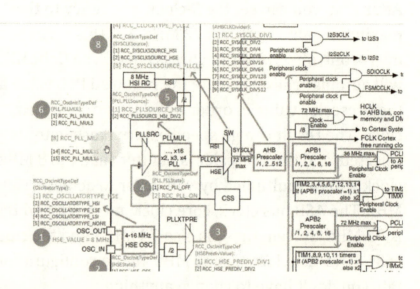

which is the high speed external, and then turn on the high speed external oscillator, and then after that select the pre-scaler to 1. The function of this line is to turn on the PLL, and then after that select the high speed external oscillator as the PLL solves, and then set the PLL multiplier to 9. These 3 line of codes is correspond to step 4, 5 and 6. In step 4, you turn on the PLL, and then select the high speed external oscillator as the PLL solves, and then select the PLL multiplier to 9. This line of codes is used to initialize the H-clocks, C-clocks, P-clocks 1 and P-clocks 2.

Then the C-clocks solves is selected from the PLL clock, and then the ASB divider is set to 1, the APB1 divider is set to 2, and the APB2 divider is set to 1. These 5 line of codes is correspond to step 7 until 11. In this step, you can select which clock that you want to initialize, which is C-clocks, H-clocks, P-clocks 1 and P-clocks 2. After that, you can select the C-clocks solves which is from PLL clock. After that, you can set the ASB pre-scaler which is 1, and then set the APB1 pre-scaler which is 2, and then set the APB2 pre-scaler which is 1. The last thing is you need to configure the flash latency.

You can go to chapter 3, and then select memory map, and select embedded flash memory, and go to reading the flash memory. Here you can see if the C-clocks value is between 48 MHz and 72 MHz, then the flash latency must be set to 2 wait stage which is correspond to this setting. This part of the codes is for configuring the C-clocks timer which I have explained it in the previous project. To verify whether the C-clocks has been set to 72 MHz or not, you can use the KL Microvision debugger. Here I add two lines of codes to get the current C-clocks frequency, and set the value in a variable called C-clocks.

After you program the STM32, you can go to debug and start debug session.

By using the debugger, you can execute your code line by line. Here you can press this button or press F10 to executing one function without entering it. You can see the control is moved from this line to this line. So this line of code has been executed. By using debugger, you can monitor the value of processor register. You can also see the value of peripheral register. For example, you can see RCC. Here you can see the RCC register and its value. And you also can see the value of variables.

For example, I will monitor the value of C-clocks variable. If this window is not shown, you can click this button, watch window. Then you can enter your variable name which is C-clocks. And then you can continue to execute the code by pressing this button. Here you can see the variable is updated. The C-clocks value is 8 MHz. This condition happens because at the startup, the default C-clocks is high speed internal oscillator which is 8 MHz. And then after you execute several line of codes, the C-clocks value is changed to 72 MHz as expected. Okay this is the end of this project.

In this project, we have learned how to configure the C-clocks using high speed external oscillator and then set the value to maximum value. You also learned how to use scale microphysic debugger to debug your code.

SOFTWARE RESET

Hi, welcome to the project number 3.2. In this project, I will teach you about software reset. So, let's get started. After finishing this project, you will be able to initiate a system reset from software and then detect the reset source by reading the reset flag. There are three types of reset in STM32. System reset, power reset, and backup domain reset. System reset will set all registers to their default values, except for reset flag and the registers in backup domain. If you look in the datasheet, you can go to software settings and then for example RCC register. And then RCC register map.

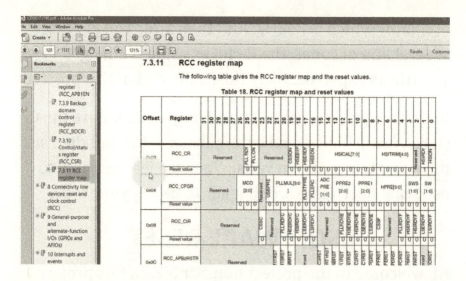

You can see every register has a reset value. So, when a system reset is occurred, all of the registers will be set to this reset value, except for the reset flag and backup domain. You can see the reset flag in this register. Here there are six reset flags. And for backup domain, you can go to chapter 5.

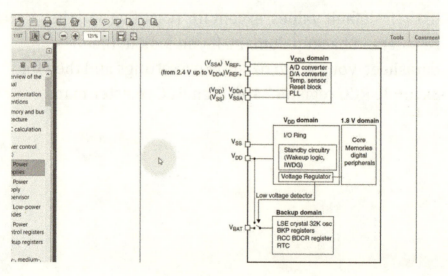

In this block diagram, you can see there is a backup domain which consists of LSE freestyle oscillator, backup register, RCC register, and RTC. When the system reset occurs, this domain will not be affected and keep its value.

Power reset will set all registers to their default values except the registers in backup domain. So, the reset flags will be affected by power reset. Backup domain reset will only set all registers in backup domain to their default values. So, other registers outside backup domain will not be affected. Other registers outside backup domain will not be affected. This is the simplified block diagram of a system reset. There are one external reset source and five internal reset sources. The external reset source is the nreset pin on STM32. To initiate a system reset from this pin, you can connect this pin to ground via a switch.

So, when you press the switch, the system reset will be occurred. For internal reset, here there is a pulse generator that will generate 20 microsecond pulse to turn on this transistor. When the transistor is on, then the system reset will be occurred.

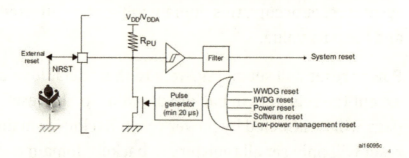

This pulse generator is triggered by one of the signals. For power reset, it will also clear the reset flag. In this project, I will explain only how to initiate the software reset. There are two sources for power reset. Power on or power down reset and when exiting the standby mode. Power on or power down reset occurs when you connect or disconnect the STM32 power supply.

For standby mode, I will explain it later in the power control project. The reset source for backup domain reset can be from backup domain software reset or when you connect the VDD or V battery to turn on the STM32. If both supplies have previously been powered off. This is because the backup domain can be powered from two power sources. So, if you disconnect only the VDD and the V battery is still connected, then the backup domain will get power from this V battery power source. This is the control status register.

36

In this register, there are 6 reset flags from bit 26 to 31. These reset flags will indicate which reset occurred, so you can initialize the system depending on the reset source.

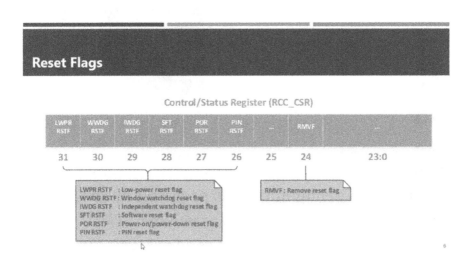

Every time you turn on the STM32, the value of these 2 reset flags, or onReset and pinReset are 1, while other flags is 0. The bit 24 can be used to clear all of these reset flags by writing 1 to this bit. You can see the detail about this register in datasheet. Ok, now I will show you how to do a software reset. Software reset is a good feature to use in case you design a product that will be placed in a place that cannot be accessed easily, so you cannot press the reset button.

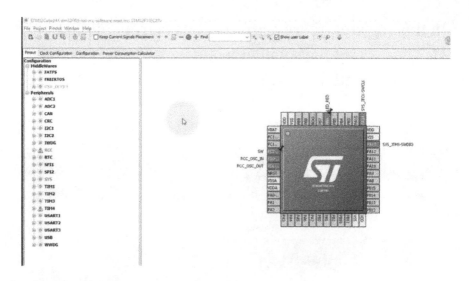

In that condition, you can do a software reset via a UART or other communication protocols by sending a specific command, so you can reset your STM32, for example from PC or other devices. In this example, I will show you how to do a software reset via a switch. In QPemX you have to enable the system debug, and then FCC for high speed external oscillator, and then you have to enable 2 GPIO pins, one for LED, which is PB6, and then the other one is for switch, which is PC15. If you see on FCC peripherals, there is an exclamation mark, if you open this, you can see that the low speed clock pin is highlighted with red color.

This is happens because the PC15 is already used for GPIO input for switch, so the PC15 cannot be used anymore for low speed external oscillator. The LED is used to indicate whether the software reset occurred or not, while the switch is used to initiate the software reset. In this step, you can set the 6 clock frequency to maximum value. In configuration step, you can go to GPIO, and then select the switch pin, and then activate the pull up resistor. After that, you can generate the code. In main.c file, you can add this code. The function of this is to read the software reset flag.

If the value of software reset is not equal to reset, it means that the software reset is occurred. Then, you can turn on the LED by using this code, and after that you can clear all the reset flag. Here, in the main loop, there is a function for read the switch. If the switch is pressed, then do a software reset. This is the result after you download the code to your STM32. For some boards, the LED may be already turned on.

This condition happens because after the code has been downloaded to STM32, Calmicrofission will do a software reset. Here, if you remember, in flash tools setting, in debug tab settings, press download, the reset and run option is enabled.

So, Calmicrofission will reset the STM32 after programming. You can press the on-board reset button to turn off the LED, and then you can press the software reset button. Here, you can see, after I press the software reset button, the LED is turned on. So, the program works as expected. Okay, this is the end of this project. In this project, you have learned how to initiate a system reset from software, and then detect a reset source by reading the reset flag.

OUTPUT CONFIGURATION

Hi, welcome to the project number 4.1. In this project, I will teach you about GPIO output configuration. So, let's get started. After finishing this project, you will be able to configure a GPIO pin in output push-pull mode and also open drain mode. The GPIO pin in STM32 can be configured to several modes – output, input, analog, and alternate function. The default mode of GPIO after reset is the input floating mode. The analog mode is used when you use the ADC or DAC peripherals, and the alternate function mode is used when you use digital peripherals like UART or timer or other digital peripherals. In this project, I will explain the GPIO output. For GPIO input, it will be explained in the next project.

There are two types of GPIO voltage in STM32, which is standard I O 3.3V and 5V tolerant I O. With 3.3 logic level pins, you can connect these pins only to a component with a 3.3 logic level, while with 5V tolerant pins, you can connect these pins either to component with 3.34 or 5V logic level. You can see whether the pins are 5V tolerant or not from the datasheet. Here, this is the datasheet of STM32 F100-103. This is not the reference manual. In this document, you can go to chapter 3 and then select this table. Here in this table, you can see a complete list of all pins for this microcontroller. This column is indicated which pin is 5V tolerant. This is the GPIO output block diagram. There is an output data register here. You can write or read a value to or from this register. The value of this register will drive the output driver depending on the mode, push-pull or open-range. And there is also other registers called bit-set or reset register. You can only write a value to this register and then the value will be transferred to output data register. But you cannot do a read operation on this register.

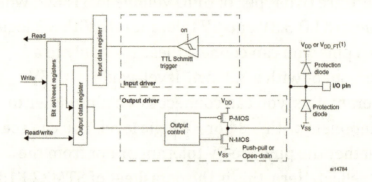

The output driver has two modes, which is push-pull or open-range. The main difference between push-pull and open-range is, in push-pull, both the PMOS and NMOS are used to control the IOPIN, while in open-range mode, only the NMOS is used to control the IOPIN. Let me show you the detail how output push-pull mode works. In push-pull mode, the logic 1 in output data register activates the PMOS, so the current can flow from VDD to the IOPIN. Suppose we connect this IOPIN to an LED, and the LED is connected to the ground. Then this LED will be ON, because the current can flow from VDD to ground. The logic 0 in output data register activates the NMOS, so the current can flow from IOPIN to the ground.

GPIO Output Open-Drain Mode

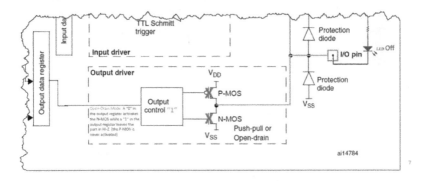

If you connect this pin to an LED, then the LED is connected to the ground, the LED will be OFF, because the current cannot flow from ground to the ground. This LED circuit is called active hype, because in order to turn on the LED, the logic value in output data register must be high of 1. Another method is to connect the LED to VDD. So, when the logic value in output data register is 0, the LED is ON, because the current can flow from VDD through the LED and then to the ground. This method is called active flow, because in order to turn on the LED, the logic value in output data register must be low of 0. When the logic value is 1, the LED is OFF, because the current cannot flow from VDD to VDD. You have seen in push-pull mode, both PMOS and NMOS can be activated depending on the logic value in output data register. Now, in open drain mode, only one transistor, which is the NMOS that can be activated. The logic 1 will not

43

activate the PMOS, so the IOPIN is in high impedance state or floating state. The logic 0 in output data register will activate the NMOS, so the current can flow from IOPIN to the ground. And then when you connect this IOPIN to an LED in active flow configuration, the LED will turn on, because the current can flow from VDD to the ground, while logic 1 in output data register will turn off the LED.

because the current cannot flow. Okay, in this demo, I will configure the GPIO output. The GPIO pin will be connected to an LED with active high configuration. First, in QPemex, you can activate the system debug, and then the RCC. After that, you can choose one GPIO, for example PB6, and then set this pin as GPIO output. And then you can name it as LED. In clock configuration tab, you can change the sysclock to the maximum value. In configuration tab, you can click the GPIO, and click this pin. In this option, you can select the GPIO mode, whether the output push pull or the output open drain.

Now I will use push pull mode, and then I will change it to open drain later. Click ok, and then you can generate the code. Here, in the main.c file, there is a function called msgpioinit, which is used to initialize the GPIO. This function will be called in this main function.

```
   167  └*/
   168  static void MX_GPIO_Init(void)
   169 ⊟{
   170
   171      GPIO_InitTypeDef GPIO_InitStruct;
   172
   173      /* GPIO Ports Clock Enable */
   174      __HAL_RCC_GPIOC_CLK_ENABLE();
   175      __HAL_RCC_GPIOD_CLK_ENABLE();
   176      __HAL_RCC_GPIOA_CLK_ENABLE();
   177      __HAL_RCC_GPIOB_CLK_ENABLE();
   178
   179      /*Configure GPIO pin Output Level */
   180      HAL_GPIO_WritePin(LED_RED_GPIO_Port, LED_RED_Pin, GPIO_PIN_RESET);
   181
   182      /*Configure GPIO pins : PC13 PC14 PC15 */
   183      GPIO_InitStruct.Pin = GPIO_PIN_13|GPIO_PIN_14|GPIO_PIN_15;
   184      GPIO_InitStruct.Mode = GPIO_MODE_ANALOG;
   185      HAL_GPIO_Init(GPIOC, &GPIO_InitStruct);
   186
   187 ⊟    /*Configure GPIO pins : PA0 PA1 PA2 PA3
   188                              PA4 PA5 PA6 PA7
   189                              PA8 PA9 PA10 PA11
   190 ┤                           PA12 PA15 */
   191      GPIO_InitStruct.Pin = GPIO_PIN_0|GPIO_PIN_1|GPIO_PIN_2|GPIO_PIN_3
   192                            |GPIO_PIN_4|GPIO_PIN_5|GPIO_PIN_6|GPIO_PIN_7
   193                            |GPIO_PIN_8|GPIO_PIN_9|GPIO_PIN_10|GPIO_PIN_11
```

To start this function, in order to use a GPIO as output, you must initialize the GPIO that you want to use. For example GPIO A, B, C, or D. And then after that, you can select the GPIO mode, which is output push pull. And then select the GPIO pin that you want to initialize, which is the LED pin.

And then after that, you can select the GPIO speed. This LED pin is defined in main.c file. Here you can see, the LED red pin is defined as GPIO pin 6, and also the LED red GPIO pub is defined as GPIO B. If you not see the main.h file, then you first must build the code. Ok, this is the step by step how to configure the GPIO. First, you can select which GPIO pin that you want to use. There is 13 GPIO modes that you can use, from alternate function, analog, interrupt, input, and output.

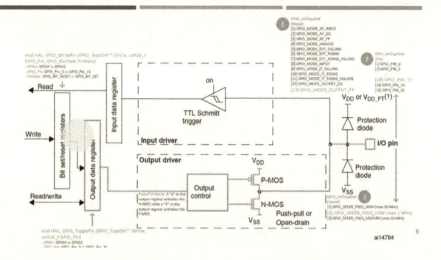

And then after that, you can select the GPIO pin that you want to initialize.

And then after that, you can set the GPIO speed, whether low speed, medium, or high speed. After that, there is 2 function that you can use to set the value of IO pin, which is GPIO toggle pin and GPIO right pin. With GPIO toggle pin, you can toggle the value of LED by reading the value from output data register, and then toggle the value, and then write the value again to the output data register. With GPIO right pin function, you can write a value to this register, bitset or register, and then the value will be transferred to output data register. You can write the value either 1 or 0 to this register.

1 is represented as GPIO bitset, while 0 is represented as GPIO bitreset. Here in the main loop, I add a code to blink the LED every 1 second. In this code, I use the

GPIO toggle pin function. This is how the program works, the LED is blinking every 1 second as expected. Now, I will show you how to modify the output mode to open VAM. You can click this button, and then select this pin. Here you can change the output mode to open VAM. Then click ok, and then you can regenerate the code. Here in the main.c file, you can see that the GPIO output mode is changed from output push pull to output open drain.

You can rebuild this code and then program the code again. This is the result, the LED is not blinking. So why this condition happens? Well, if you remember, when the GPIO is in output open drain mode, the PMOS is never activated. Even when the logic in output data register is 1, so the current never flow to the LED. Therefore, the LED blinking is not work. To make this code work, you must change the CV to active flow. So when the value in output data register is 1, the current can flow from VDD to the ground. Ok, this is the end of this project. In this project, you have learned how to configure a GPIO pin in output push pull mode and open drain mode.

INPUT CONFIGURATION

Hi, welcome to the project number 4.2. In this project, I will teach you about GPIO input configuration. So let's get started. - After finishing this project, you will be able to configure a GPIO pin in input pullup mode, pulldown mode, and floating mode.

There are three digital logic values, which is HIGH or logic 1, and then LOW or logic 0, and then FLOATING, or sometimes called twisted high impedance or high Z. The floating value occurs when the pin is not pulled to a high or low logic level. The floating pin can be seen as an open shift bit or a floating wire. The floating pin can be in a high or low logic value, or in between high and low logic value. So the microcontroller might unpredictably interpret the input value as either a logical high or logical low. This is happens simply because if there is external electrical noise on that pin, the pin will oscillate.

This problem can be solved by pulling the pin to a high or low logic value via a pullup or pulldown resistor. So the logic value of the pin is well defined under all conditions. A pullup or pulldown resistor is used when the GPIO pin is in input mode. As you can see here in this picture, this is the pullup resistor and this is the pulldown resistor.

This resistor is called pullup resistor because the resistor is connected to the VCC, while this resistor is called pulldown resistor because this resistor is connected to the ground.

 When you configure the GPIO pin as output open drain, you also need a pullup resistor. Because when you configure in output open drain, the pMOS transistor is never activated. So you cannot produce high value to the IO pin, instead the output pin has a high impedance state.

Pull-Up and Pull-Down Resistors

- A pull-up/down resistor is used when the GPIO pin is in input mode.
- Output open-drain mode also needs a pull-up resistor.

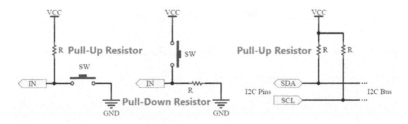

So the pullup resistor will give the logic one to the IO pin. One of example where pullup resistor is necessary is on I2C bus pins. Pullup or pulldown resistor can be an internal or external component. In STM32 there are internal pullup and pulldown resistor on every pin. Here for example in STM32 F103 and here in STM32

F407. Here in F1 you can see the pullup and pulldown resistor is located inside the input driver.

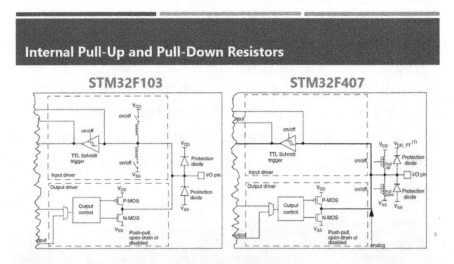

So this pullup and pulldown resistor can be used only when the GPIO is configured as input mode. You cannot use this pullup resistor or pulldown resistor when the GPIO is configured in output mode.

In STM32 F4, the pullup and pulldown resistor is located outside the input driver. So it means that you can use this pullup or pulldown resistor when you configure the GPIO in input mode as well as in output mode.

This is the block diagram of GPIO pin when configured in input pullup mode. Here there is an input data register that will store the value of GPIO pin. So the software can read the IO pin state by reading this register. In this mode, the pullup resistor is activated.

So the current can flow from VDD to Schmitt trigger. And the default value of the input data register is a logic 1. Suppose you have a switch that connected to this pin. Then when you press the button, the current will flow from VDD to the ground via pullup resistor. So the input data register value is now 0.

This circuit is called active flow, because when the button is pressed, the microcontroller will read this condition as logic 0 instead of 1. This is the GPIO block diagram when the GPIO pin is configured in input pulldown mode. The pulldown resistor is activated so the current can flow from Schmitt trigger or from IO pin to the ground. Then the default value of the input data register is logic 0. Suppose you have a switch that connected to this pin, then when you press the switch, the current will flow from VDD to Schmitt trigger and also to the pulldown resistor.

So the input data register value is now 1. This circuit is called active height, because when the button is pressed, the microcontroller will read this condition as logic 1 instead of 0.

This is the GPIO block diagram when the GPIO pin is configured in input floating mode. Because of neither pull up nor pull down resistor is activated, so the default value of the input data register is a floating value. If you configure the GPIO pin in input floating mode then you must add an external pull up or pull down resistor. So the default value of input data register is well defined. In this example, I connect the GPIO input pin with an external pull up resistor and a switch.

GPIO Input Floating Mode

So when the switch is not pressed, the current from VDD will flow to the Schmitt trigger.

Therefore, the input data register receives a logic 1. When the button is pressed, the current from VDD will flow to the ground. Therefore, the input data register receives a logic 0. This result is the same as when use an internal pull up resistor. Okay, in this demo, I will show you how to initialize a GPIO in input mode. First, you have to enable the system debug peripera. And then the RCC pin. After that, you can select one GPIO, for example PC15 and then enable this pin as GPIO input. You can name it as switch because this pin will be connected to the switch using active low shift quick.

And then you can enable one more GPIO for LED to indicate when the switch is pressed, then the LED will turn on. In this case, I choose the PB6. In clock configuration tab, you can change the clock to the maximum value. In configuration tab, you can click GPIO and then you can configure the pin for output, whether you want to use push pull or open drain. And then for pin put, in this option, you can select whether you want to use the pull up resistor, pull down resistor or nothing. Here in this example, I will choose the pull up resistor. After that, click ok and then you can generate the code.

In main.c file, in mxgpio init function, here there is a code for initialize the GPIO. In this code, you can see the switch pin is initialized as GPIO input mode with a pull up resistor. This is the step by step how to initialize the GPIO. This step is the same as when you initialize the GPIO as output mode in the previous project. First, you have to select which GPIO mode that you want to use, which is GPIO mode input in this case. And then after that, you can choose which GPIO pin that you want to initialize. And then you can select the pull up or pull down resistor configuration.

After that, in order to read the value from input data register, you can use this function called GPIO read pin. And when the value inside the input data register is 1, this function will return GPIO bit reset. While when the value inside the input data register is 0, then this function will return GPIO bit reset. Here in this line, there is initialization code for GPIO output which is connected to the LED. The output mode is output push pull. And then there are also another initialization for example for GPIO A and GPIO B. This initialization code is for unused GPIO pin which is initialized as GPIO analog mode. This is happens because if you remember in QPemex, here in project, settings, code generator tab, there is an option for set all 3 pins as analog to optimize the power consumption. Because this option is enabled, so in GPIO init function, all 3 pins will be initialized as analog. Here in main loop, I add code for reading the switch set. When the switch is pressed which is equal to reset or 0, then you must turn on the LED. Otherwise the LED is off. This is how the program works. When I press the switch, the LED is on.

And then when I release it, the LED is off.

So the program works as expected. Okay this is the end of this project. In this project we have learned how to configure a GPIO pin in input pull up, pull down, and floating mode.

EXTERNAL INTERRUPT CONFIGURATION

Hi, welcome to the project number 5. In this project, I will teach you about external interrupt configuration. So let's get started. After finishing this project, you will be able to configure a GPIO pin in input mode with interrupt mode. First, before I go to external interrupt configuration, I would like to make sure you are aware of the concept of interrupt and how it is different from polling. Well, polling is the process when the processor periodically checks its peripheral to see if it needs service or not. The analogy for polling is when you check your phone periodically, for example every one minute, to see if someone is calling you or not.

On the other hand, interrupt is the process when the processor can do any tasks and the peripheral will interrupt the processor when it needs service. The analogy for interrupt is that you can do what you want and the phone will ring to interrupt you when someone is calling. The concept of polling and interrupt can best be explained by an example. In SysTick timer project, there's a simple program that consists of LED and switch. The LED is blinking for every 3 seconds, which is the red LED, and then whenever the switch is pressed, the yellow LED will turn on.

```
96     /* Infinite loop */
97     /* USER CODE BEGIN WHILE */
98     while (1)
99     {
100    /* USER CODE END WHILE */
101
102    /* USER CODE BEGIN 3 */
103        /* Toggle red LED every 3s. */
104        HAL_GPIO_TogglePin(LED_RED_GPIO_Port, LED_RED_Pin);
105        /* When the CPU is executing this delay code, the CPU just waits for
106         * 3s and not do anything. */
107        HAL_Delay(3000);
108        /* Process that has a long computation time */
109
110        /* If button is pressed. */
111        if (HAL_GPIO_ReadPin(SW_GPIO_Port, SW_Pin == GPIO_PIN_RESET)
112        {
113            /* Turn on yellow LED. */
114            HAL_GPIO_WritePin(LED_YELLOW_GPIO_Port, LED_YELLOW_Pin, GPIO_PIN_SET);
115        }
116        else
117        {
118            /* Turn off yellow LED. */
119            HAL_GPIO_WritePin(LED_YELLOW_GPIO_Port, LED_YELLOW_Pin, GPIO_PIN_RESET);
120        }
121    }
122    /* USER CODE END 3 */
123
```

You also learn how to make this button more responsive by using a non-blocking delay. But it's still a polling method because the processor must regularly check the switch every 3 seconds. Suppose you have a process that have a long computation time that replace this delay process. Then you cannot use the non-blocking delay to make the switch more responsive, because with the real process, the processor must do a computation. Then the only way to make this switch responsive is to use interrupt. So you don't have to check the switch regularly and when the switch is pressed, interrupt controller will interrupt processor to suspend this process, and then execute the code inside the interrupt service routine, in this case to turn on the LED.

After that, the processor can back to this process to execute this process again. There are two types of interrupt, which are external and internal interrupt. External interrupt is generated from external peripherals, for example push button, rotary encoder and etc. Internal interrupt is generated from internal peripherals, for example ADC, timer, UART, etc. This is the block diagram of external interrupt.

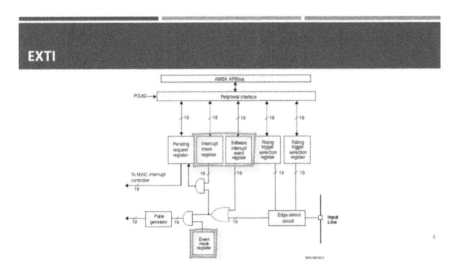

Here there is an input line, this input line is connected to edge detector circuit to detect whether rising edge or falling edge or both edge occurred, and that edge will be used as a trigger to generate interrupt of event.

The difference between event and interrupt is when event occur, it doesn't execute an interrupt service routine. It just generates a pulse to indicate there is an event occurred. Event can be used in order to wake up the processor from sleep or stop mode. I will explain it later in the power control project. When an interrupt occurs, it will be stored in a pending request register. And then, the NVIDIA interrupt controller can select which interrupt must be served first in case there are two or more pending interrupts. The detail about NVIDIA will be explained in the next project.

Here there are also software interrupt register and interrupt marks or event marks register. The function of software interrupt register is to trigger this external interrupt from software, and the function of interrupt or event marks register is to enable or disable the interrupt of event. The external interrupt can be triggered by rising edge, falling edge or both edge. Rising edge is a transition from logic 0 to logic 1. When interrupt is configured in this mode, then whenever there is a transition from 0

the interrupt is occurred. On the other hand, falling edge is a transition from logic 1 to 0. When interrupt is configured in this mode, then whenever there is a transition from 1 to 0, the interrupt is occurred.

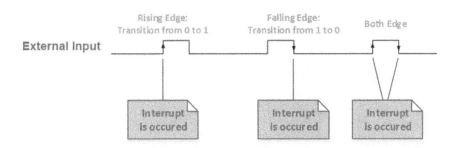

When interrupt is configured in both edge mode, then whenever there is a transition from 0 to 1 and 1 to 0, the interrupt is occurred. Ok, let me show you how to configure external interrupt in cubeMX. First, enable the System Debug peripheral, and then the RCC. After that, enable 2 pins as GPIO output for red and yellow LED, and then enable 1 pin as GPIO input with external interrupt mode for switch.

So, whenever the switch is pressed, then the external interrupt will be generated in order to turn on or off the yellow LED. The function of red LED is only for blinking every 3 seconds. In clock configuration tab, you can set the sysclock frequency to the maximum value. In configuration tab, click the GPIO. You can set the GPIO mode for LED, either push pull or open band depending on your circuit. And then you can select this pin, and then you can select the GPIO mode, which is external interrupt mode with rising and falling edge feature detection. Don't forget to enable the pull up or pull down resistor, and then click ok.

After that, go to the Envig settings, and then don't forget to enable this interrupt which is for the switch, then click ok. After that, you can generate the code. Here, in the main.c file, in mxgpio init function, this function is the same like when you configure the GPIO input in previous project. The difference is only in the GPIO mode, where interrupt rising and falling edge is selected, and at the end of this function, here there is code for set the interrupt priority, and then enable the interrupt. I will explain how to configure this interrupt priority in the next project.

For now, you can use this default priority. Here, in the main.look, I add code for blinking the red LED for every 3 seconds. And then, you can open the stm32f1sx-it. This file contains all the interrupt service routine. Here, there is an external interrupt service routine for exti line 10 to 15, which is the switch is connected to line 15. In this function, you can place the code for reading the switch. So, whenever the switch is pressed, the yellow LED is on, otherwise it is off. This is how the program works. The red LED is blinking every 3 seconds. When I press the switch, the yellow LED will turn on.

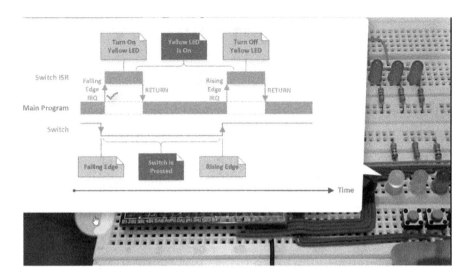

The falling edge interrupt is occurred. The processor will suspend the execution of main program in order to execute the code inside interrupt service routine, which is to turn on the LED. Then, after that, processor will back again to continue the execution of main program. When I release the switch, the rising edge interrupt is occurred. Processor will suspend the execution of main program in order to execute the code inside interrupt service routine. Which is to turn off the LED. And then, after that, processor will back again to continue the execution of main program. Okay, this is the end of this project. In this project, you have learned how to configure a GPIO pin in input with interrupt mode.

INTERRUPT PRIORITY CONFIGURATION

Hi, welcome to the project number 6. In this project, I will teach you about interrupt priority configuration. So let's get started. After finishing this project, you will be able to configure interrupt preemption priority and interrupt sub-priority. Here in reference manual, and then go to and pick interrupt controller. Here there is a table that list all available interrupt factors. Every interrupt has a set table priority except for 3 days interrupt. The function of and pick or nested factored interrupt controller is to manage all of these interrupt factors based on its priority.

10	17	settable	EXTI4	EXTI Line4 interrupt	0x0000_0068
11	18	settable	DMA1_Channel1	DMA1 Channel1 global interrupt	0x0000_006C
12	19	settable	DMA1_Channel2	DMA1 Channel2 global interrupt	0x0000_0070
13	20	settable	DMA1_Channel3	DMA1 Channel3 global interrupt	0x0000_0074
14	21	settable	DMA1_Channel4	DMA1 Channel4 global interrupt	0x0000_0078
15	22	settable	DMA1_Channel5	DMA1 Channel5 global interrupt	0x0000_007C
16	23	settable	DMA1_Channel6	DMA1 Channel6 global interrupt	0x0000_0080
17	24	settable	DMA1_Channel7	DMA1 Channel7 global interrupt	0x0000_0084
18	25	settable	ADC1_2	ADC1 and ADC2 global interrupt	0x0000_0088
19	26	settable	CAN1_TX	CAN1 TX interrupts	0x0000_008C
20	27	settable	CAN1_RX0	CAN1 RX0 interrupts	0x0000_0090
21	28	settable	CAN1_RX1	CAN1 RX1 interrupt	0x0000_0094
22	29	settable	CAN1_SCE	CAN1 SCE interrupt	0x0000_0098
23	30	settable	EXTI9_5	EXTI Line[9:5] interrupts	0x0000_009C
24	31	settable	TIM1_BRK	TIM1 Break interrupt	0x0000_00A0

So for example, if there are 2 or more pending interrupts occur at the same time, then the and pick will choose which interrupt will be served first. There are 2 types of interrupt priority, preemption priority and sub-priority. For preemption priority, if an interrupt has a higher preemption priority than another interrupt, then this interrupt can preempt the execution of another interrupt. Level 0 is the highest preemption level. For sub-priority, if there are 2 or more pending interrupts with the same preemption priority level, then sub-priority level is used to determine which pending interrupt must be served first.

NVIC Priority Type (cont.)

Level 0 is the highest sub-priority level. These 2 types of interrupt priority can best be explained by an example. Here this is an example for preemption priority. In this example, there are main, program and 2 interrupt service routines.

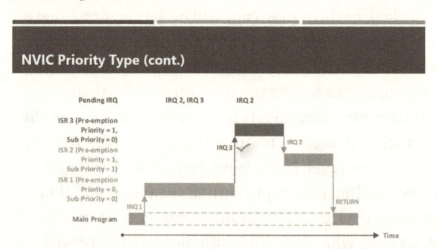

Interrupt service routine 1 is preemption priority 1, while interrupt service routine 2 is preemption priority 0, which is the highest level. Also interrupt service routine 2 can preempt the execution of interrupt service routine 1. Here when the interruptrequest1 is occurred, then the execution of main program is suspended in order to execute the interrupt service routine 1.

When interruptrequest2 is occurred, then the execution of interrupt service routine 1 is suspended in order to execute the interrupt service routine 2. After interrupt service routine to finish, then processor will beg to execute the interrupt service routine 1. And then finally after interrupt service routine 1 finish, the processor will beg to execute the main program. Here another example for explaining the sub-priority. In this example, there are main program and 3 interrupt service routine. Interrupt service routine 1 has preemption priority 0, while interrupt service routine 2 and 3 has preemption priority 1.

And then, interrupt service routine 2 has sub-priority 1, while interrupt service routine 3 has sub-priority 0, which is the highest sub-priority level. So, when pending interrupt request 2 and 3 occur at the same time, then interrupt service routine 3 will be served first. Here, when the interrupt request 1 is occurred, then the execution of main program is suspended in order to execute the interrupt service routine 1. Suppose at this time, there are 2 interrupt requests, interrupt request 2 and 3 that occur while processor is executing interrupt service routine 1.

These 2 interrupts cannot preempt the interrupt service routine 1, because interrupt service routine 1 has higher preemption priority level than interrupt service routine 2 and 3. Therefore, interrupt service routine 2 of 3 will be executed after interrupt service routine 1 finishes. The interrupt request 3 will be executed first after the interrupt service routine 1 finishes, because this interrupt request has a higher sub-priority than interrupt request 2. And finally, after interrupt service routine 3 finishes, the interrupt request 2 will

The Envig Priority Group is used to determine how many priority levels are valuable for preemption level and sub-priority level. For STM32F103, there are 5 priority groups from 0 to 4. In Priority Group 0, there are 0 bits for preemption priority and 4 bits for sub-priority. So there is only 1 preemption level available and 16 sub-priority level available. In Group 1, there are 1 bit for preemption priority and 3 bits for sub-priority. So there are 2 preemption level and 8 sub-priority level available. In Group 2, there are 2 bits for preemption priority and 2 bits for sub-priority.

So there are 4 preemption level and 4 sub-priority level. In Group 3, there are 3 bits for preemption priority and 1 bit for sub-priority. So there are 8 preemption level and 1 sub-priority level available. Finally, in Group 4, there are 4 bits for preemption priority and 0 bit for sub-priority.

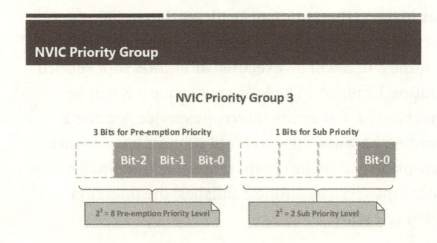

NVIC Priority Group

NVIC Priority Group 3

So there are 16 preemption level available and 0 sub-priority level. Okay let me show you how to configure the intra preemption and sub-priority. Here in CubeMX, you can enable the system debug and then the RCC. After that, we have to set 3Gpio as output for LED.

In this case, I use PB6, PB7 and PB8 for red, yellow and green LED. And also 3 more GPIO as input with external interrupt mode for 3 switches. In this case, I use PC13, PA1 and PA2. You can choose another pin for external interrupt input, but you must choose pins that have different interrupt service routine. Here in reference manual in chapter 10, external interrupt, you can see that every GPIO pin can be connected to external interrupt line, but through a multiplexer. So it means that if you already configured the external interrupt 0 to PA0, then you cannot use external interrupt 0 for PB0, PC0 and so on.

And then in interrupt vector, here you can see EXTI line 0 to 4 has its own interrupt service routine. But for EXTI line 5 to 9, the interrupt service routine is shared and also for EXTI line 10 to 15. Therefore, for this example, you must choose all GPIO pins that has its own interrupt service routine, because you have to set different priority for each switch. Here the EXTI line 13 is correspond to this interrupt service routine, and then EXTI line 1 and 2 is correspond to these two interrupt service routine. So all of the pins has its own interrupt service routine.

Therefore, you can set different priority to each switch. In clock configuration tab, you can set the sqf frequency to the maximum value. In configuration tab, go to GPIO, and then you can configure the GPIO mode for the LED. After that, you can configure the GPIO mode for switches, which is I use the external interrupt mode with rising S3 chip detection. And then after that, don't forget to enable the pull up or pull down resistor. In this case, I will use pull up resistor. Click ok, and then go to NVID. Here you must enable 3 interrupt service routine, which is for EXTI line 1, line 2, and EXTI line 10 to 15.

EXTI line 10 to 15 is used for switch 0, line 1 is used for switch 1, and line 2 is used for switch 2.

Here in this options, you can select the npc priority group. In this case, I use priority group 3. And then after that you have to set the preemption priority, which is switch 0 has preemption priority of 3, switch 1 is 2 and switch 2 is 1.

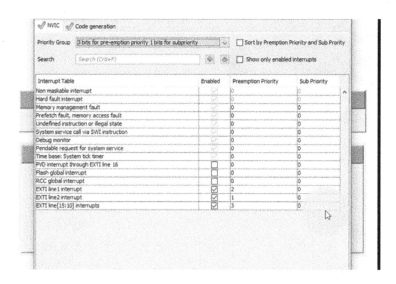

For now, I will leave all sub-priority to 0. And then later, I will modify this configuration. Click ok, and then generate the code. Here in main loop, you don't have to add anything, because I will place the code inside the interrupt service routine. You can open this file, stm32f1.xxtintrap. This file contains all of the interrupt service routine that you use in your project.

Here there are 3 interrupt service routine for exti line 1. Line 2 and line 10 to 15, which is correspond to switch 1, switch 2 and switch 0 respectively.

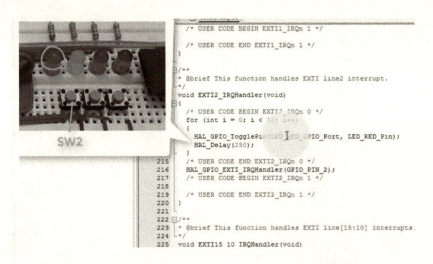

```
/* USER CODE BEGIN EXTI1_IRQn 1 */

/* USER CODE END EXTI1_IRQn 1 */
}

/**
* @brief This function handles EXTI line2 interrupt.
*/
void EXTI2_IRQHandler(void)
{
    /* USER CODE BEGIN EXTI2_IRQn 0 */
    for (int i = 0; i < 10; i++)
    {
        HAL_GPIO_TogglePin(LED_GPIO_Port, LED_RED_Pin);
        HAL_Delay(250);
    }
215     /* USER CODE END EXTI2_IRQn 0 */
216     HAL_GPIO_EXTI_IRQHandler(GPIO_PIN_2);
217     /* USER CODE BEGIN EXTI2_IRQn 1 */
218
219     /* USER CODE END EXTI2_IRQn 1 */
220 }
221
222 /**
223  * @brief This function handles EXTI line[15:10] interrupts.
224  */
225  void EXTI15_10_IRQHandler(void)
```

SW2

And inside this interrupt service routine, there are codes for blinking the LED several times. If I press the switch 0, then the green LED will blink. If I press the switch 1, then the yellow LED will blinking. And if I press the switch 2, then the red LED will blinking. This is how the program works. First, I will press the switch 0, and then switch 1, and finally switch 2, and see what will happen.

If I press the switch 0, then the green LED will blink. For another example, I will press switch 1, and then switch 0, and finally switch 2. Now, I will show you another example how to use interrupt sub-parameter.

Go to NVID, change the preemption priority for switch 0 to 2, and sub-priority for switch 1 to 1. So now switch 0 and switch 1 has the same preemption priority level. Therefore, they cannot preempt each other.

The function of sub-priority is to determine which interrupt will be served first from pending interrupt state. In this case, switch 0 has the highest sub-priority level. So switch 0 will be served first from pending step. Click ok, and then regenerate the code. After I download the code, this is how the program works. First, I will press switch 2, and then switch 1, and finally switch 0, and see what will Ok, this is the end of this project. In this project, we have learned how to configure the interrupt preemption priority and sub-priority.

MEMORY-TO-MEMORY MODE

Hi, welcome to the project number 7. In this project, I will teach you how to configure DMA in memory to memory mode. So, let's get started. After finishing this project, you will be able to configure DMA to move data from flash memory to embedded sram memory. First before I go to DMA configuration, I would like to make sure you are aware of what is DMA or Direct Memory Access. Well, DMA is a feature which allows data transfer between memory and memory, or memory and peripheral, or peripheral and peripheral without the help of CPU. So the DMA transfer not use CPU resource.

Of course, you can easily move data with the CPU. So why do you need the DMA for data transfer? Using the CPU for data transfer is perfectly fine if you only interested in transferring a small number of bytes. But what if you would like to transfer a large amount of data continuously? For example, when you want to interfacing with the graphic LCD module where the pixel data has to be sent over and over, this Mac CPU will be see only for this task. So it will be nice if we use DMA to transfer a large amount of data and only allow the CPU if necessary when the transfer is finished.

Therefore, it freeze up the CPU for other tasks while the data is being transferred by DMA. Effectively, the microcontroller is multitasking. STM32F103 has 2 DMA, DMA1 and DMA2.

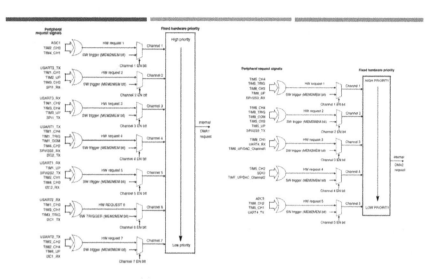

This is the block diagram of DMA1 and DMA2. The DMA1 has 7 channels and DMA2 has 5 channels. Channel 1 has the highest hardware priority while channel 7 or channel 5 in DMA2 has the lowest hardware priority. Each of the channel is mapped to several peripherals. The requests from peripherals such as timer, ADC or UART are connected to the ORB gate before entering the DMA. This means that only one request must be enabled at a time.

The DMA request can be triggered either from hardware or from software. The mode when DMA is triggered from software is called memory to memory mode. Each of DMA channel has a priority. An arbiter is used to manage the DMA channel request. The arbiter manages the channel request based on that priority and launches the memory of peripheral access sequences. There are 4 levels of software priority that can be programmed to each channel. Hardware priority is used when there are 2 or more requests that have the same priority level. The channel with lowest number will get priority versus the channel with the highest number.

For example, if channel 2 and 4 have the same software priority, then channel 2 will get priority over channel 4. In the device with 2 DMA, the DMA1 request has priority over DMA2 request. Each DMA channel has a capability to generate an interrupt on these 3 events as transfer, transfer complete or transfer error. Okay in this demo, I will show you how to configure DMA in memory to memory mode. The program will do a data transfer from flash memory to extra memory by using DMA. In QPAMX, you can configure the system debug and then the FCC. After that, you can enable 2 GPIO as output for example PB6 and PB8.

These 2 GPIO are used for red and green LED. This LED will be used to indicate that the transfer data is correct or not.

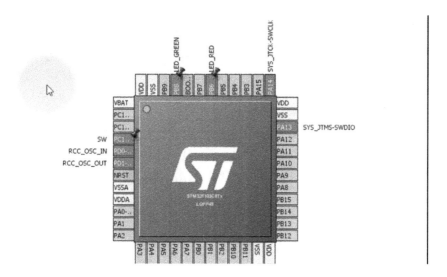

And then you need to enable 1 GPIO pin as input for switch. This switch will be used to start the DMA data transfer. In clock configuration tab, you can set the sysclock to maximum value. In configuration tab, click GPIO, here you can configure the GPIO mode for output pin and also for input pin. After that, go to DMA, go to memory to memory tab.

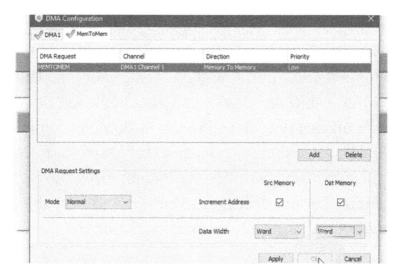

Here you can add a new DMA request and select memory to memory. Set the data width to work and then click ok.

After that, you can generate the code.

In main.c file, there is a function called mxDMAInit. This function is generated by QPemex for initialize the DMA. Now I will add my code.

```
main.c
50    /* Private variables ------------------------------------------------*/
51    #define BUFFER_SIZE 32
52
53    /* store array data in FLASH memory */
54    const uint32_t srcBuffer[BUFFER_SIZE] =
55    {
56      0x01020304, 0x05060708, 0x090A0B0C, 0x0D0E0F10,
57      0x11121314, 0x15161718, 0x191A1B1C, 0x1D1E1F20,
58      0x21222324, 0x25262728, 0x292A2B2C, 0x2D2E2F30,
59      0x31323334, 0x35363738, 0x393A3B3C, 0x3D3E3F40,
60      0x41424344, 0x45464748, 0x494A4B4C, 0x4D4E4F50,
61      0x51525354, 0x55565758, 0x595A5B5C, 0x5D5E5F60,
62      0x61626364, 0x65666768, 0x696A6B6C, 0x6D6E6F70,
63      0x71727374, 0x75767778, 0x797A7B7C, 0x7D7E7F80
64    };
65    uint32_t dstBuffer[BUFFER_SIZE];
66    /* USER CODE END PV */
67
68    /* Private function prototypes ------------------------------------*/
69    void SystemClock_Config(void);
70    static void MX_GPIO_Init(void);
71    static void MX_DMA_Init(void);
72
73    /* USER CODE BEGIN PFP */
74    /* Private function prototypes ------------------------------------*/
75    uint8_t BufferCmp(uint32_t* pBuff1, uint32_t* pBuff2, uint16_t len);
```

First you have to add these two arrays that have 32 elements, soft buffer and destination buffer. The soft buffer is initialized with constant keyword. So it means that this array is stored in the flash memory instead of SRAM. After that you can add this function prototype. This function will be used for comparing the content of soft buffer and destination buffer. And here this is the definition for buffer compare function.

And then in main loop, you have to add these codes.

76

```
113     /* Infinite loop */
114     /* USER CODE BEGIN WHILE */
115     while (1)
116     {
117     /* USER CODE END WHILE */
118
119     /* USER CODE BEGIN 3 */
120        /* DMA transfer */
121        /* Wait for user button press before starting the transfer */
122        while (HAL_GPIO_ReadPin(SW_GPIO_Port, SW_Pin) == GPIO_PIN_SET);
123
124        /* Start the DMA transfer using polling mode */
125        HAL_DMA_Start(&hdma_memtomem_dma1_channel1, (uint32_t)&srcBuffer,
126             (uint32_t)&dstBuffer, BUFFER_SIZE);
127
128        /* Polling for transfer complete */
129        HAL_DMA_PollForTransfer(&hdma_memtomem_dma1_channel1,
130             HAL_DMA_FULL_TRANSFER, 1000);
131
132        /* Compare the source and destination buffers */
133        if(BufferCmp((uint32_t*)srcBuffer, (uint32_t*)dstBuffer, BUFFER_SIZE))
134        {
135           /* Turn red LED on */
136           HAL_GPIO_WritePin(LED_RED_GPIO_Port, LED_RED_Pin, GPIO_PIN_SET);
137        }
138        else
```

The function of this code is to read the switch and wait until the switch is pressed. After that this code will start DMA to transfer data from flash to SRAM by using polling mode. And then in this line you have to wait until the transfer process is finished. Finally in this line, the contents of destination buffer will be compared to soft buffer. If the contents are matched then the green LED will be on, otherwise the red LED will be on. After that you can build the code. In this build output window, there is information about program size.

I will copy this to notepad. Program size is consist of code, read-only data, read-write data and uninitialized data. Code and read-only data are stored inside the flash memory while read-write data and uninitialized data is stored inside the SRAM. And then I will change this variable. I will remove the constam keyword and let's see what will happen. Let's build the code. This is the result. I will copy this to notepad. Here you can see the size of read-only data and read-write data are different. The difference is 128 bytes which correspond to the size of soft buffer variable.

This happens because when you not use the constam keyword, the soft buffer variable is stored inside the SRAM instead of flash memory. This is the result. When I press the switch, the green LED is on which indicates that the data is successfully transferred from soft buffer to destination buffer by using DMA.

Now I will show you another example how to configure the DMA with interrupt. In kube-mx, the DMA configuration is the same as the previous example. And then you have to go to npick. You have to enable this DMA1 channel 1 global interrupt. Click ok and then you can regenerate the code.

Here this part of the code is the same as the previous example. In function prototype you can add this function. This function will be called after DMA transfer is completed. In main loop you can add this code. First you have to wait until the switch is pressed and then start the DMA transfer in interrupt mode. Here the most important thing. In mxdma-ini function you have to add this line of code. The function of this code is when the DMA transfer is completed then the transfer complete function will be called inside the interrupt service routine. And here you can see that the DMA1 channel 1 interrupt is enabled by kube-mx.

And finally this is the buffer compare function which is the same as the previous example. And then this is the definition for transfer complete function. In this function the contents of source buffer and destination buffer is compare if max then turn on the green led otherwise they create led. The result is the same as previous example when using polling method. When I press the switch the green led is on which indicates that the data is successfully transferred. Ok, this is the end of this project. In this project you have learned how to configure DMA in memory to memory mode.

POLLING MODE AND DATA TYPE CONVERSION

Hi, welcome to the project number 8.1. In this project, I will teach you how to configure UART in polling mode and how to do a data type conversion for UART transmission. So let's get started. After finishing this project, you will be able to configure UART transmitter and receiver in polling mode and convert integer and real number to string for UART transmission. As we know, UART is stands for Universal Asynchronous Receiver Transmitter.

UART Data Frame

- Data bit (**5, 6, 7, 8, 9 bits**), Start bit, Stop bit (**1, 1.5, 2 bits**), Parity bit (**None, Even, Odd**), Baud rate (**9600, 19200, 115200 bps**)

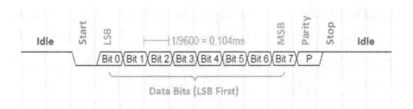

UART is commonly used for interfacing between microcontroller and PC or microcontroller to another module. Because it is asynchronous, then there are only data lines, which are TX line for transmit and RX line for receive.

UART is basically just a digital circuit that converts parallel data to serial data on the transmitter side and converts serial data to parallel data on the receiver side. This is the UART serial data frame. Each of the data frame can consist of 5 to 9 data bits with LSB first configuration. The commonly used data bits is 8 bits or 1 byte. When there is no data or idle condition, TX and RX line is always 1. And then there is a start bit and stop bit which are indicate where the first and the last data bit. The start bit is always 0 and this stop bit is always 1.

The length of stop bit can be selected either 1, 1.5 or 2 bits. The parity bit is an optional bit that can be used to detect error. The parity bit can be even or odd parity. There are several standard for baud rate such as 9.6 kbps or 19.2 kbps or 115.2 kbps. For example if the baud rate is 9.6 kbps, then the period of 1 bit is about 0.104 ms. This is an example for UART data frame when sending or resetting the ASCII A character. The data frame setting is 8 and 1, which means 8 data bits, no parity and 1 stop bit. Here the LSB of ASCII A will be sent first after the start bit.

The logic 1 and 0 of UART data frame can be represented by using several voltage representation. For example TTL which means 5V for logic 1 and 0V for logic 0.

Voltage Level

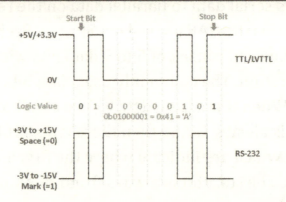

And there is also LTTL or low voltage TTL which means logic 1 is 3.3V and logic 0 is 0V. Another commonly used voltage level is RS232. In this logic level 0 is represented as positive voltage between plus 3V and plus 15V and 1 is represented as negative voltage between minus 3V and minus 15V.

Voltage Level Conversion

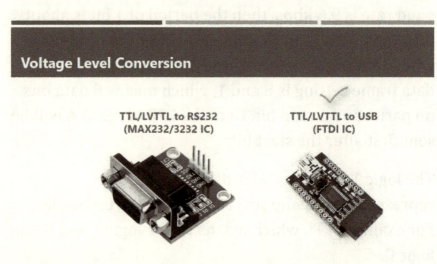

Because of there are several voltage for UART, then you must know which voltage level that is used on your device.

In case for STM32, the voltage level is L3 TTL or 3.34. And then to connect your STM32 to PC, you need a voltage level converter. If you use PC that has DB9 port on your motherboard, then you can use this module to convert from L3 TTL to RS232 voltage. This kind of module is usually used MAX232 IC for TTL or MAX3232 IC for L3 TTL. If you use a laptop or your PC doesn't have a DB9 port, then you can use L3 TTL to USB converter module which is usually based on FTDI IC. This is the connection diagram from your STM32 to PC.

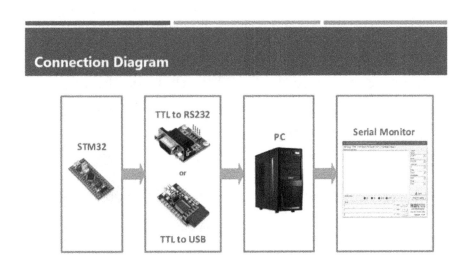

Connection Diagram

There are 3 pins that must be connected from your STM32 to your 4 test converter module which are TX, RX and GND.

The TX and RX are cross connected, which means that the TX of the STM32 is connected to the RX of converter module and the RX of STM32 is connected to the TX of converter module. From some module, the TX pin might be labeled as RX and RX is labeled as TX. So you should check this if your converter module doesn't transmit or receive anything to or from PC. And then in PC, you should use a serial monitor software in order to write or read data from or to your STM32.

Ok, in this demo, I will show you two examples. In example 1, I will show you how to configure UART in polling mode. And in example 2, I will show you how to convert integer and real number to string for UART transmission. Ok, let's begin with example 1. In this example, I will show you a simple program for turn on and turn off an LED from PC. In QPIME X, you can configure the system debug and then the RCC. After that, you can enable the UART. In this case, I will use UART 2. Select the mode to asynchronous. And then after that, we have to configure one GPIO as output or LED.

In clock configuration tab, you can set the clock to your desired value.

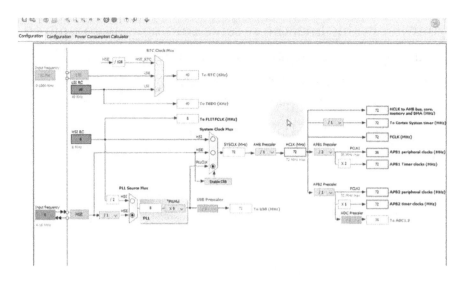

In configuration tab, you can go to GPIO and then you can set your GPIO mode. After that, you can go to UART. In this window, you can configure the Baud rate, data bits, parity bits, and stop bits. For this example, I will use the default settings. Click ok. And then you can generate the code. Here in my.g file, I have marked all of the codes that I have added to this project. You can add or remove this mark by using this button or by pressing Ctrl F2. Here you have to add a library, string.h.

And then here you can add two array variables. This array is declared with constant keyword so it will be stored in flash memory instead of SRAM. And then here in my loop, this line is used to transmit the initial message to PC with 1ms timeout. After that, this line is used to receive data from PC with 5 seconds timeout. So you have 5 seconds to enter the command from your PC. In this line, the receive command is compared by using string compare function. If the command is equal to LED1, then turn on the LED and also transmit this message to PC. If the command is equal to LED0, then turn off the LED and also transmit this message to PC.

Here there is also function called strlen. This function is used to get how many bytes does the message variable has. The strlen and string compare function is defined in string.h library. This is the result. In serial monitor, this initial message will be printed every 5 seconds.

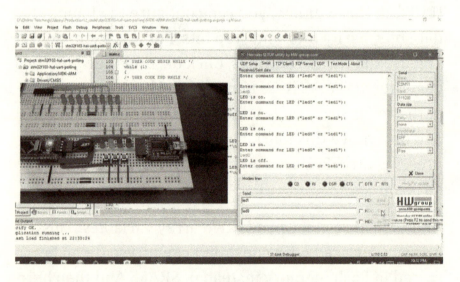

When I send the LED1 command, the LED will be on and this message will be printed which indicates that the LED is on. And then when I send the LED0 command, the LED will be off and the LED is off status will be printed. Okay in example 2, the cubeMX configuration is the same as previous example.

In main.c file, you can add these codes if there are two numbers integer and real that will be sent to PC by using UART. But before that, we must convert this data type integer and double to array of characters because this function, how UART transmit can only transmit characters not integer nor double. In order to do that, you have to create a buffer that will store the characters for example str buffer and then by using this function, sprintf, the integer number will be converted to array of characters.

```
 90
 91    /* Initialize all configured peripherals */
 92    MX_GPIO_Init();
 93    MX_USART2_UART_Init();
 94
 95    /* USER CODE BEGIN 2 */
 96    int intValue = 168;
 97    double realValue = -168.888;
 98    char strBuffer[16];
 99
100    sprintf(strBuffer, "%d\n", intValue);
101    HAL_UART_Transmit(&huart2, (uint8_t *)strBuffer, strlen(strBuffer), 1);
102
103    sprintf(strBuffer, "0x%X\n", intValue);
104    HAL_UART_Transmit(&huart2, (uint8_t *)strBuffer, strlen(strBuffer), 1);
105
106    sprintf(strBuffer, "%.2f\n", realValue);
107    HAL_UART_Transmit(&huart2, (uint8_t *)strBuffer, strlen(strBuffer), 1);
108    /* USER CODE END 2 */
109
110    /* Infinite loop */
111    /* USER CODE BEGIN WHILE */
112    while (1)
113    {
114      /* USER CODE END WHILE */
115
116      /* USER CODE BEGIN 3 */
```

This format %d is for integer number in decimal. Here another example to print this number to hexadecimal by using %x format to convert real number.

You can use %f format for example %.2f which means that the real number will be rounded to two decimal places. This sprintf function is defined in string.x library. This is the result. After you download and run the code, the numbers will be printed to serial monitor. This is the integer number in decimal and this is in hexadecimal and this is the real number that has been rounded to two decimal places. Okay this is the end of this project. In this project, you have learned how to configure UART in polling mode and how to do a data type conversion for UART transmission.

INTERRUPT MODE, RX FIFO BUFFER, AND DMA MODE

Hi, welcome to the project number 8.2. In this project, I will teach you how to configure UART in interrupt mode and then create a file for buffer for resaving data. And finally, I will show you how to configure UART in DMA mode. So let's get started. After finishing this project, you will be able to configure UART transmitter and receive data in interrupt mode and then receive data in interrupt mode by using RS-50 buffer. And then configure UART transmitter and receiver in DMA mode. So in order to do that, I will show you 3 example projects. This is the example one.

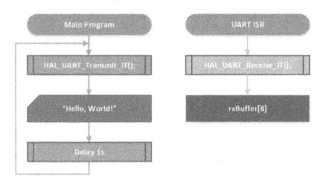

In this example, I will create a simple program to transmit and receive data by using UART in interrupt mode. This program consist of main program and UART interrupt service routine. In main program, this text Hello Web will be sent every 1 second to PC by using UART transmit IP function. And then whenever there is an incoming character in UART data register, the UART interrupt service routine will be occur. Once set the interrupt service routine, this function UART receive IP will be called to receive the character and then save the received character in the RS buffer variable.

Here in cubeMX, the configuration is the same as previous example. Except for this example, I will not use any LED. In UART configuration, you have to enable the UART global interrupt and then click OK. And then you can generate the code. Here in my.c file, you can add this variable for receiving data. Here in this line, you have to enable the UART rxNOTEMPTY interrupt. So whenever there is an incoming character in UART data register, the UART interrupt will be occur. Here in these two lines, the Hello Web string will be sent to PC every 1 second by using UART in interrupt mode.

After that you can open this file, the interrupt file.

```
17    *      may be used to endorse or promote products derived from this software
18    *      without specific prior written permission.
19    *
20    * THIS SOFTWARE IS PROVIDED BY THE COPYRIGHT HOLDERS AND CONTRIBUTORS "AS IS"
21    * AND ANY EXPRESS OR IMPLIED WARRANTIES, INCLUDING, BUT NOT LIMITED TO, THE
22    * IMPLIED WARRANTIES OF MERCHANTABILITY AND FITNESS FOR A PARTICULAR PURPOSE ARE
23    * DISCLAIMED. IN NO EVENT SHALL THE COPYRIGHT HOLDER OR CONTRIBUTORS BE LIABLE
24    * FOR ANY DIRECT, INDIRECT, INCIDENTAL, SPECIAL, EXEMPLARY, OR CONSEQUENTIAL
25    * DAMAGES (INCLUDING, BUT NOT LIMITED TO, PROCUREMENT OF SUBSTITUTE GOODS OR
26    * SERVICES; LOSS OF USE, DATA, OR PROFITS; OR BUSINESS INTERRUPTION) HOWEVER
27    * CAUSED AND ON ANY THEORY OF LIABILITY, WHETHER IN CONTRACT, STRICT LIABILITY,
28    * OR TORT (INCLUDING NEGLIGENCE OR OTHERWISE) ARISING IN ANY WAY OUT OF THE USE
29    * OF THIS SOFTWARE, EVEN IF ADVISED OF THE POSSIBILITY OF SUCH DAMAGE.
30    *
31    ************************************************************************
32    */
33    /* Includes ---------------------------------------------------------*/
34    #include "stm32f1xx_hal.h"
35    #include "stm32f1xx.h"
36    #include "stm32f1xx_it.h"
37
38    /* USER CODE BEGIN 0 */
39    extern char rxBuffer[8];
40    /* USER CODE END 0 */
41
42    /* External variables -----------------------------------------------*/
43    extern UART_HandleTypeDef huart2;
```

In this file, you have to add the rxbuffer variable but with external keyword. Because this variable is already required outside this file which is in my.c file. And then in UART interrupt handler, you must add this code in order to receive data and save the data in rxbuffer variable. After that you can build and download the code. This is the result. I will run the program in debug mode in order to see the content of rxbuffer. I will run this program. Here you can see the contents of rxbuffer are zero.

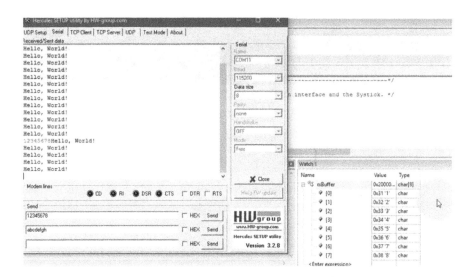

And the Hello Web is printed every 1 second. And then I will send this data. Here you can see the data is received in rxbuffer while the Hello Web is being transmitted. Ok in example 2, I will create a receive FIFO buffer. This buffer will be filled with an incoming character from UART data register with interrupt mode. So whenever there is an incoming character in UART data register, then the rxNodeEmpty interrupt will be occur in order to move this character from UART data register to this buffer. After that I will add one switch.

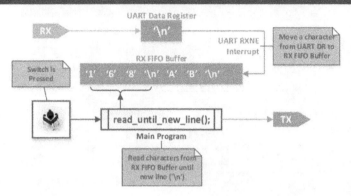

Whenever I press the switch, the main program will take all of the characters from FIFO buffer until newline character and transmit that data back to PC. So the main program will wait until the newline character is found, then transmit all of the characters including this newline character to the PC. In KubeMX, the configuration is the same as previous example except for this example I will add one GPIO pin for switch. In configuration tab, don't forget to configure the pull up or pull down resistor for the switch. And then in UART configuration, don't forget to enable the UART global interrupt.

After that, in generate the code. Here in main.c file, in this line, you can add the string.h library. Then in this line, you can declare your FIFO buffer that has 64 elements. This two variable is used for width and right pointer. And then this variable is used to indicate how many characters inside the FIFO buffer. And then this variable rxOverflow is used to indicate if the buffer is overflow or not. These two variables are declared with volatile keyword because these two variables will be modified in main program and interrupt service routine. So whenever you create a variable that will be modified in main program as well as in interrupt service routine, you must use volatile keyword.

Here you can add function prototag for reading one character from the FIFO buffer. Here in this line, this is the definition for rxBufferGetChar function. This function will read one character from FIFO buffer. And then increment the width pointer and after that, increment the rxCounter. And then after that, you can go to the interrupt file. These are the variable declarations. These variables are the same with the declaration in main.c except with extern keyword.

```
195    void USART2_IRQHandler(void)
196  {
197        /* USER CODE BEGIN USART2_IRQn 0 */
198
199        /* USER CODE END USART2_IRQ
200        //HAL_UART_IRQHandler(&huart
201        /* USER CODE BEGIN USART2_IR
202        if (__HAL_UART_GET_IT_SOURCE(          , UART_IT_RXNE))
203        {
204            /* Write an incoming char to buffer */
205            rx_buffer[rx_wr_index] = huart2.Instance->DR;
206
207            /* Increment write pointer */
208            rx_wr_index++;
209            if (rx_wr_index >= RX_BUFFER_SIZE)
210            {
211                rx_wr_index = 0;
212            }
213
214            /* Increment char counter */
215            rx_counter++;
216            if (rx_counter >= RX_BUFFER_SIZE)
217            {
218                rx_counter = 0;
219                rx_overflow = 1;
220            }
221        }
```

And then in UART interrupt handler, you can add these codes and also you have to comment or delete this line of code that generated by kubemx.

In this line, every incoming data in UART data register will be stored in the rxBuffer. Then increment the width pointer and also the rxCounter. And then I will back to main.c file. Here in main loop, the function of this line is to wait until the switch is pressed and then this code is used to read all of the characters in FIFO buffer until newline character. And then this line will transmit all of the characters until newline back to the PC. This is the result. I run the program in debug mode and monitor the value of rxBuffer. Here I open the serial monitor and then I will send several characters from serial monitor.

Here you can see the characters are saved in FIFO buffer. And then I will press the switch. The first data is printed. Press it again. The second data is printed. Press it again. The third data is printed. Ok this is the example 3. In this example, I will configure UART in DMA mode. I will create a program that will generate a waveform from a lookup table that stored inside the flash memory. The waveform data will be sent to PC by using UART in DMA mode. First, the program will transmit these text.

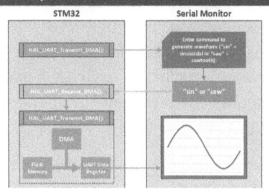

from STM32 to Serial Monitor by using DMA. And then you can enter whether you want to generate a sinusoid wave or sawtooth wave by entering one of these commands. The command will be received by using UART in DMA mode. After that, the waveform data from transmemory will be transferred to UART by using DMA. The UART will transmit the data to Serial Monitor. In CubeMX, you have to continue UART and then enable the UART Global Interrupt. And also you have to enable DMA. Here the DMA request for UART RX and UART TX. The transmitter mode is set to normal and then later I will show you the circular mode.

Click ok and then generate the code. Here in main.c, this is the initial message and then this sinusoid and sawtooth lookup table. These variables will be stored inside the slash memory because this variable is declared with constant keyword. Here in main.program, this line will transmit the initial message by using UART in DMA mode. These two lines will receive data by using UART in DMA mode and wait until the data is received. After that, these lines will transfer the waveform data from slash memory to UART depending on the received command either sinusoid or sawtooth.

This is how the program works. I will send sign to the STM32. And then after that you can see the sinusoid data will be printed. You can visualize this data by using Microsoft Excel. Here this is the result. Now I will change the DMA mode to circular mode. I will change from the code inside this file. STM32F1.xx half msp.c. You can open this file from this folder. Actually you can change the code from QPIMX and then regenerate the code. But for now I will show you how to change directly from the code. Then you can change the mode to circular mode. And then I will go back to main.cfile and then I will change this code in order to transmit the initial message without using DMA.

And then you can rebuild the code. This is the result. I will generate sinusoid. And then here you can see the waveform is printed to serial monitor continuously. We can visualize this in excel. This is the result.

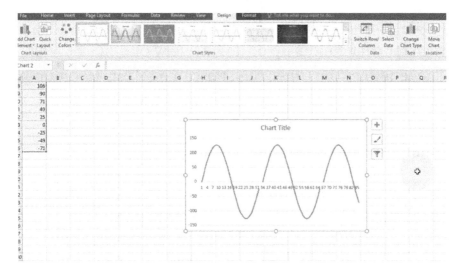

So the conclusion is when you configure DMA in circular mode then the DMA will transfer the data from one memory location to another memory location continuously. Ok this is the end of this project. In this project you have learned how to configure UART in interrupt and DMA mode and also how to create a FIFO buffer for UART receiver in interrupt mode.

TIME BASED INTERRUPT AND ENCODER INTERFACE MODE

Hi, welcome to the project number 9.1. In this project, I will teach you how to configure a timer to generate an interrupt and then configure a timer in encoder interface mode. So let's get started. After finishing this project, you will be able to configure a timer to generate an interrupt request and then configure a timer in encoder interface mode in order to read a

97

rotary encoder. Ok, as we know, a timer is just a register that counts up or down every one clock cycle. The length of the timer register can be 8 bit, 16 bit or even 32 bit. For up counting timer, when the register reach the maximum value, for example 255 in 8 bit timer, then the value will overflow to zero.

00:00:57 - For down counting timer, when the register reach the minimum value, then the value will underflow to 255 in case of 8 bit timer. This is the timing diagram of an 8 bit timer. The overflow signal is set to 1 when the counter value goes from 255 to 0.

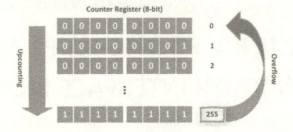

From this diagram, you can know that the duration of the period of one timer count is equal to the period of the timer clock. So the counter period is 1 divided by timer clock frequency. For example, if the timer clock is equal to CPU clock which is 72 MHz, then the counter period is 1 divided by 72 MHz which is equal to 13.88 nanosecond.

And then, if you know the counter period, then you can calculate the maximum duration for this timer by multiplying the counter period with 256 because it is 8 bit timer. When you configure a timer, you usually need to configure a prescaler value. Well, a prescaler is used to slow down the timer clock frequency.

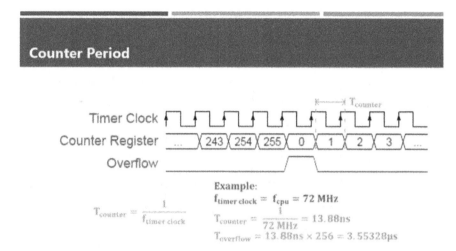

Counter Period

Timer Clock

Counter Register ... 243 254 255 0 1 2 3 ...

Overflow

$T_{counter}$

Example:
$f_{timer\ clock} = f_{cpu} = 72\ MHz$

$T_{counter} = \dfrac{1}{f_{timer\ clock}}$

$T_{counter} = \dfrac{1}{72\ MHz} = 13.88ns$

$T_{overflow} = 13.88ns \times 256 = 3.55328\mu s$

Here in this timing diagram, you can see a timer with the prescaler of 2. With this setting, the counter register will be incremented every 2 internal clock cycles, so the duration of one count is more longer than without prescaler. Therefore, the overflow duration is also longer than without prescaler.

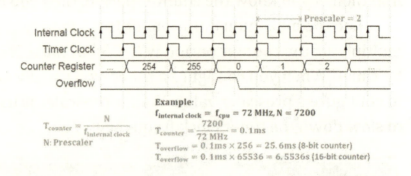

For example, if I use the prescaler equal to 7200, then the counter period is equal to 7200 divided by internal clock frequency which is 72 MHz. So the result is 0.1 millisecond. With this counter period value, you can count up to 25.6 milliseconds for 8 bit timer or 6.5 seconds for 16 bit timer. Ok, in the previous slide, the counter register of a timer is always incremented every fixed period from internal clock. Another configuration that usually used is the counter mode. In counter mode, the counter register can be incremented every external event such as rising edge, falling edge, or both edge.

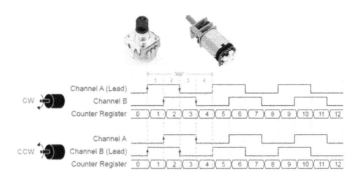

So the counter period is not fixed. In counter mode, the counter register is incremented asynchronously, while in timer mode, the counter register is incremented synchronously. One example of counter mode is the encoder interface mode. In this mode, the counter register will count up or down when the rotary encoder rotates. This type of encoder has two outputs, channel A and channel B. And then every transition on each channel will increment the counter register. There are 4 counts, every one mechanical tick. So this encoder is usually called quadrature encoder.

You can also determine the direction of the rotation by determine which channel is leading. For example, if channel A is leading, then you can assume that this direction is clockwise. So when channel B is leading, then it is counterclockwise rotation. In this demo, I will show you two examples. In example 1, I will configure a timer to generate an interrupt every 1 second. And in example 2, I will configure a timer to rotate a rotary encoder. For example 1, in QPemex, as usual, you have to configure the system debug and then the RCC. After that, you can configure the timer one and select the clock source from internal clock.

And then you can enable one GPIO pin for LED. The LED will be toggled every 1 second from timer interrupt. After that, go to clock configuration.

and then go to configuration. you can configure the GPIO of the LED and then after that configure the timer one. here you can set the pre-scaler to 7200 minus one. minus one is because it is start from zero instead of one. I choose the pre-scaler to be 7200 because my sql value is 72 megahertz and I want to get 10 kilohertz for my timer one clock. then with 10 kilohertz in order to achieve one second overflow you can set the reload value to be 10,000 minus one. so the interrupt will be occur whenever the timer one overflow which is every one second. after that go to and click settings and then you can enable the timer one update interrupt. click OK and then you can generate the code. this is the main.c file. here is the function for stop the timer one in interrupt mode and then in main loop you don't have to add anything and then in this line this is the function that will be called inside the timer interrupt service routine.

inside this function there is a code of toggling the LED. then you can open the interrupt file. here is the timer one interrupt handler that has been generated by QPyMX. you can right click on this line of code and then click go to definition of this function. here in this line these codes are for timer update interrupt and the how timer period elapsed callback is called here. this function is already declared in this file.

```
    main.c     stm32f1xx_it.c     stm32f1xx_hal_tim.c
2830              HAL_TIM_IC_CaptureCallback(htim);
2831        }
2832        /* Output compare event */
2833        else
2834        {
2835              HAL_TIM_OC_DelayElapsedCallback(htim);
2836              HAL_TIM_PWM_PulseFinishedCallback(htim);
2837        }
2838        htim->Channel = HAL_TIM_ACTIVE_CHANNEL_CLEARED;
2839      }
2840    }
2841    /* TIM Update event */
2842    if(__HAL_TIM_GET_FLAG(htim, TIM_FLAG_UPDATE) != RESET)
2843    {
2844      if(__HAL_TIM_GET_IT_SOURCE(htim, TIM_IT_UPDATE) !=RESET)
2845      {
2846          __HAL_TIM_CLEAR_IT(htim, TIM_IT_UPDATE);
2847          HAL_TIM_PeriodElapsedCallback(htim);
2848      }
2849    }
2850    /* TIM Break input event */
2851    if(__HAL_TIM_GET_FLAG(htim, TIM_FLAG_BREAK) != RESET)
2852    {
2853      if(__HAL_TIM_GET_IT_SOURCE(htim, TIM_IT_BREAK) !=RESET)
2854      {
2855          __HAL_TIM_CLEAR_IT(htim, TIM_IT_BREAK);
2856          HAL_TIMEx_BreakCallback(htim);
```

you can right click and go to definition of this function. this function is declared with weak attribute so it means that you can and should override this function in main.c file because this function should not be modified here. after that you can build and then download the code. this is the result the LED is blinking for every one second as expected.

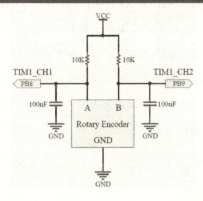

in example 2 I will show you how to configure timer for reading the rotary encoder. this is the rotary encoder circuit that I will use in this example. this rotary encoder is connected to PA8 and PA9 which are the input pin for timer one in encoder interface mode. these are the pull up resistors and base capacitors are used to avoid the bouncing. here in QPyMX you can enable the system debug and then the FCC. after that enable one uav of sending the encoder count to PC and then enable timer one in encoder mode.

after that go to configuration tab. here you can configure the timer one. you can set the counter period to FF so after 255 the counter will go back to 0. and then in encoder section you can set the polarity of channel 1 to rising edge and channel 2 to falling edge. click OK and then generate the code.

104

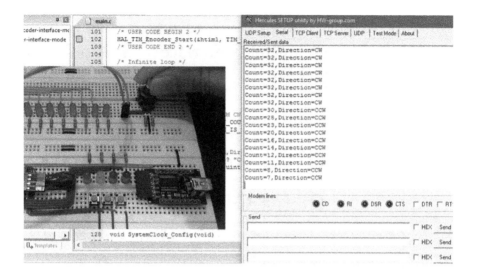

in mine.c file you have to add the string.s library and then add these three variables. here the function of this line is to stop the timer in encoder mode and then in mine loop this line will get the counter value from timer one counter register and then store in encoder count variable. this code will read the direction of rotary encoder either clockwise or counterclockwise. and then finally this line of codes will send the encoder count to the PC by using uav. after that you can build and download the code. this is the result. the encoder count and its direction is printed to the serial monitor. then I will rotate the encoder.

the encoder value is incremented and the direction is clockwise. when I refer the direction then the encoder value is decremented and the direction is counterclockwise. okay this is the end of this project. in this project you have learned how to configure timer to generate an interrupt every one second and then configure a timer in encoder interface mode in order to read the rotary encoder.

OUTPUT COMPARE TOGGLE AND PWM OUTPUT

Hi, welcome to the project number 9.2. In this project, I will teach you how to configure a timer in output compatible and in PWM output mode. So, let's just start it. After finishing this project, you will be able to configure your STM32 to generate a square wave signal and then generate a PWM signal. Ok, in the previous project, you have learned two useful modes of timer. First is for generating a time-based interrupt and then the second is the encoder interface mode.

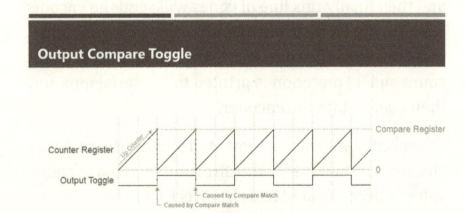

In this project, I will show you another useful mode

which is output compare mode. Output compare mode is work by comparing the counter register value against one or two value in other registers.

And then when the value are matched, then a digital output is set to logic high, low or toggled. In this example, I will show you two examples. In example 1, I will configure the timer in output compare toggle mode. So, the digital output of a GPIO pin will be toggled whenever the counter register value is matched to the compare register value. So, the result is a square wave signal with 50% duty cycle. Actually, we can do this by using timer interrupt, as we did in the previous project. But the difference is when you use timer interrupt, the GPIO pin is toggled by software.

You must use the HAL GPIO toggle function. But when you use timer output compare toggle, the GPIO pin is toggled by the timer hardware. So, you will not use the HAL GPIO toggle function. Okay, in QPemx, you have to enable the system debug and then the RCC. After that, you can enable one timer.

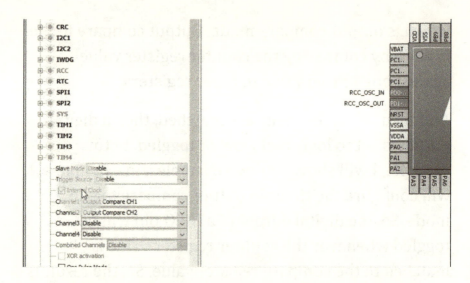

For example, I am using timer 4, enable the internal clock, and then enable to output compare channel 1, and then output compare channel 2. The timer for channel 1 is connected to the red LED, while the timer for channel 2 is connected to the yellow LED. After that, go to configuration.

Set the 6 clock value to 72 MHz, and then go to configuration, and then configure the timer for.

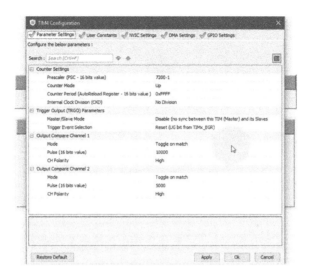

Set the 3 scalar value to 7200, and then set the contact period to the maximum value. After that, set the output compare mode to toggle on mix, for channel 1, and also for channel 2. And then set the initial compare match value for channel 1 to 10000, and for channel 2 to 5000. After that, go to config settings, and enable the timer for global interrupt. Click ok, and then you can generate the code. Here in main.c file, in this line, you can add these two line of codes for starting the timer for channel 1 and channel 2 in output compare mode.

Here in this line, you have to add this callback function. This callback function will be called inside the interrupt service routine when the compare match is occurred.

```
271      * @retval None
272      */
273   void HAL_TIM_OC_DelayElapsedCallback(TIM_HandleTypeDef *htim)
274   {
275      uint32_t capture = 0;
276
277      /* TIM4 CH1 toggling with frequency = 1 Hz */
278      if(htim->Channel == HAL_TIM_ACTIVE_CHANNEL_1)
279      {
280         capture = HAL_TIM_ReadCapturedValue(htim, TIM_CHANNEL_1);
281         /* Set the capture compare register value */
282         __HAL_TIM_SET_COMPARE(&htim4, TIM_CHANNEL_1, (capture + 10000));
283      }
284
285      /* TIM4 CH2 toggling with frequency = 2 Hz */
286      if(htim->Channel == HAL_TIM_ACTIVE_CHANNEL_2)
287      {
288         capture = HAL_TIM_ReadCapturedValue(htim, TIM_CHANNEL_2);
289         /* Set the capture compare register value */
290         __HAL_TIM_SET_COMPARE(&htim4, TIM_CHANNEL_2, (capture + 5000));
291      }
292   }
293   /* USER CODE END 4 */
294
295   /**
296      * @brief  This function is executed in case of error occurrence.
297      * @param  None
298      * @retval None
```

If the channel 1 value is matched, then you must set the new compare value, which is the current value, plus 10000. The same as channel 1 for channel 2, if the value is matched, then you must set the new compare value, which is the current value, plus 5000. So the fatality of the timer for channel 1 will be toggling every 1 second.

and then yellow LED or timer for channel 2 will be toggling every 0.5 seconds. After that, you can build and download the code. This is the result. The red LED which is correspond to channel 1 is toggling every 1 second. And the yellow LED which is correspond to channel 2 is toggling every 0.5 seconds. Ok, in example 2, I will show you how to configure the output compared in PWM mode. The main difference between toggle mode and PWM is, in toggle mode, the duty cycle of square wave signal is fixed to 50%. But in PWM mode, you can configure the duty cycle between 0 to 100%.

Another difference between toggle mode and PWM mode is, in toggle mode, the output signal is changed only when the counter value is matched to the compare value. But in PWM mode, the output signal is changed when the counter value is matched to the compare value and also to the counter overflow value. Ok, in QPemex, you can set the timer for inter-magnetic clock and channel 2 to PWM generation. This GPIO pin, timer for channel 2 is connected to the yellow LED. After that, go to clock configuration tab. Here I set the sysclock frequency to 72 MHz and then go to configuration.

You can configure the timer for. Set the prescalar value to 18. So, the timer clock is 72 MHz divided by 18 which is 4 MHz. So, the counter value is incremented every 1 divided by 4 MHz which is 0.25 microsecond. After that, you can set the reload value of the counter period to 124. So, the PWM resolution is 10 bit. With the timer clock frequency and counter reload value information, you can calculate the PWM signal period which is timer clock period multiplied by counter reload value. 0.25 microsecond multiplied by 1024 is 256 microsecond. So, this is the PWM signal period and the PWM frequency is about 3.9 kHz.

After that, set the PWM mode to mode 1 and then enable the fast mode. In unfixed settings, you don't need to enable the interrupt. Click ok and then generate the code. In main.c file, in this line, you have to stop the timer in PWM mode for channel 2. In main loop, I will create a simple program for increase and decrease the LED intensity. The PWM value or the compare value will be incremented or decremented by 50 every 50 milliseconds from 0 to 1024. This is the result. The LED intensity is gradually changed from fully off to fully on and then back to fully off. Ok, this is the end of this project. In this project, you have learned how to configure timer in output compare toggle and PWM output mode.

INPUT CAPTURE AND PWM INPUT

Hi, welcome to the project number 9.3. In this project, I will teach you how to configure a timer in input capture mode and PWM input mode.

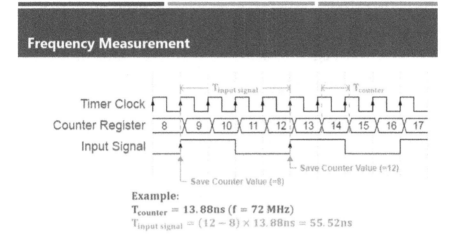

Frequency Measurement

Example:
$T_{counter} = 13.88ns$ (f = 72 MHz)
$T_{input\ signal} = (12 - 8) \times 13.88ns = 55.52ns$

So, let's get started. After finishing this project, you will be able to configure your STM32 to measure the square wave signal frequency and then measure the PWM signal frequency and also the duty cycle. Input capture mode is used for capturing the times of events such as rising and falling eggs. The counter register is in rerunning mode. It means that the counter value will count from 0 to maximum value and then back to 0 and count again over and over.

When an event occurs, then the counter register value will be saved. The input capture mode can be used for measuring the frequency of a digital signal. In this project, I will show you two examples. In example 1, I will configure the timer in input capture mode to measure the frequency of a square wave signal. And then in example 2, I will configure timer in PWM input mode to measure both the frequency and the duty cycle of a PWM signal. This is the example 1. In this example, the timer is configured in input capture mode. The counter register will count from 0 to maximum value over and over.

And then whenever there is a rising egg on input signal, then the counter register value will be saved. With two successive capture values, you can calculate the duration for one cycle of this signal which is 12 minus 8 and with the counter clock period information, you can calculate the period of the input signal. Then if you know the period of input signal, you can also calculate the frequency. Here in QPAMX, I will configure timer 3, timer 4 and UF2. Timer 3 is used for input capture while timer 4 is used to generate a PWM output signal. This PWM output signal will be used as an input for the input capture pin of the timer 3.

The UF2 is used for sending the frequency value to the PC. In timer 3, enable the internal clock and then enable the channel 1 in input capture mode. In timer 4, enable the internal clock and then enable the PWM generation mode. After that, go to clock configuration, reset the clock value to 7 MHz and then go to configuration, configure the timer 4, set the rescaler to 18 and the period to 1024. This is the same setting as in the previous project. So if you calculate the frequency of the PWM signal, the result is about 3.9 kHz. Here you can set the PWM mode 1 and then you can enable the fast mode.

Set the pulse to 384 so the duty cycle is 37.5%. Click ok and then configure the timer 3 in input capture mode. Set the reload value of the counter-predator value to the maximum value. And then after that you can set the polarity selection to raising H. So whenever there is a raising H on input pin, the counter value will be saved. After that, go to nfig settings and then enable the timer global interrupt.

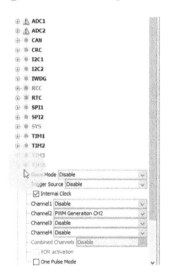
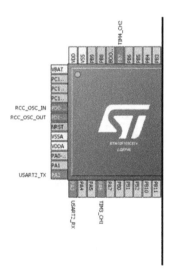

The interrupt will be off-cured whenever the counter value is captured. Click ok and then you can generate the code. In mine.c file, add the string.h library and then add these variables for storing the first and second capture value, the difference and then the frequency.

- In this line, you must start the timer 4 in PWM mode and then in this line you must start the timer 3 in input capture mode. In main loop, the code will transmit the frequency value to PC every 2 seconds by using UART. And then here in this line, there is a capture callback function. This function will be called inside the interrupt service routine. Here we save the first input capture value. After that, here we save the second input capture value. And then we can calculate the difference. And finally, we can calculate the frequency.

This is the result, I connect the PWM output pin of timer 4 to the input capture pin of timer 3. Then, I open the serial monitor.

Here the frequency is printed to the serial monitor. The frequency is exactly the same as we calculate before. Ok, in example 2, I will configure a timer in PWM input mode. In this mode, the frequency and duty cycle of PWM signal can be measured. In this mode, two input capture channels is used. Channel 1 is configured to capture counter value FV rising edge and channel 2 is configured to capture counter value FV falling edge.

Unlike in previous example, in this example, the counter value is reset to 0 FV rising edge with the timer slave mode. So we don't need to capture two successive values for calculating the signal period. FV falling edge, the counter value will be saved in order to calculate the duty cycle with this formula. You have to add 1 to the capture value because the counter register is start from 0. Max, you have to enable the timer 3, timer 4 and UART 2. Timer 3 will be configured in PWM input mode and timer 4 will be configured in PWM output mode. This PWM output signal will be used as an input for the PWM input pin of the timer 3.

In timer 4, enable the internet log and the PWM mode on channel 2. mode. So we don't need to capture two successive values for calculating the signal period. So we don't need to capture two successive values for calculating the signal period. We only need to calculate the frequency and duty cycle. Open the serial monitor.

POLLING MODE AND INTERRUPT MODE

Hi, welcome to the project number 10.1. In this project, I will teach you how to configure ADC in polling mode and also in interrupt mode. So let's get started. After finishing this project, you will be able to configure your ADC to perform single confection in polling mode and then configure ADC to perform single continuous confection in interrupt mode. Ok as we know ADC or analog to digital converter is used to convert analog voltage to a digital value.

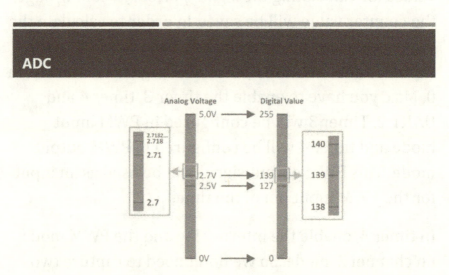

In mathematics, it is said that the analog voltage consists of an infinite number of points between point A and point B. In this example between 0 volts and 5 volts.

Here for example after 2.74 there are axis 2.71, 2.718, 2.7182 and so on. But a microcontroller can only represent a finite set of numbers or usually called discrete numbers. For example, 8 bit number can only represent numbers from 0 to 255. In this example between 139 and 140 there is no other number. So the function of an ADC is to map the infinite number of points, for example between 0 and 5 volts to the finite number of points. For example between 0 and 255. When an analog voltage says 2.71 volts then it will be represented as 139. The analog value is simply bounded to the nearest value of the digital number.

Ok this is the reference manual of STM32F1. This is the ADC block diagram. The STM32F1 has 3 ADC peripherals. The ADC is connected to up to 16 external channels and 2 internal channels.

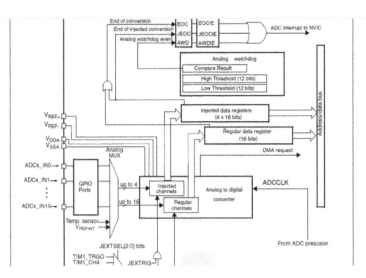

The internal channel is used for measuring the internal temperature and reference voltage. There are 2 types of channels, regular channel and injected channel. The difference between regular and injected is the injected channel can interrupt the regular channel conversion. And also the injected channel has a dedicated ADC data register for up to 4 injected channels. The ADC conversion can be started from software and also from hardware, for example timer trigger.

After analog to digital conversion finish, then the ADC can generate an interrupt or a DMA request. There is also an analog washdog feature that can monitor if the analog voltage is exceeding or within the predefined upper and lower threshold. Ok in STM32 there are several ADC conversion modes, single, single continuous, scan, scan continuous and discontinuous mode. Single mode will convert only one channel in single shot or continuous mode. Scan mode will convert a set of predefined channel in single shot or continuous mode. Continuous mode will convert only one channel at each trigger from a set of predefined channels.

In this project I will show you how to configure ADC in the single mode, in polling mode and also in single continuous mode in interrupt mode.

ADC Conversion Modes

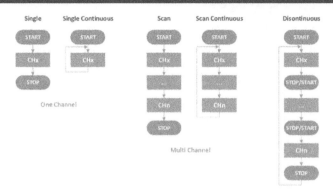

For scan mode it will be explained in the next project. Ok for example one, in cubeMX you can enable the system debug after that the RCC and then you have to enable one UART, for example UART2. This UART will be used to send the ADC value to the PC and then after that go to ADC1. Here you can enable one ADC channel, for example I use the channel 6, but you can use other channels if you want. This channel 6 is correspond to PA6.

and this pin will be connected to a potentiometer. after that you can go to clock configuration. here i set the cc value to 72MHz. and then after that go to configuration.

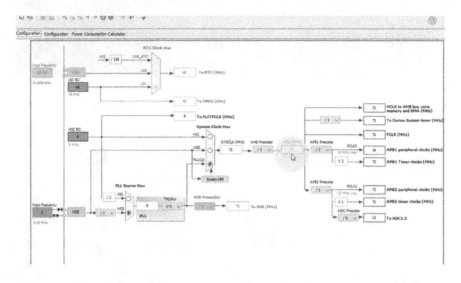

here you can configure the ADC one. for now i will not change any settings. just use the default settings. click ok. and then after that you can generate the code. ok here is the main.c file. in this line you can add the string.h library. and then add these two variables. here i add one function prototype called abcread. this function will do a single abc conversion in point mode. and then after that in main loop this code will do a single abc conversion.

and then convert the result to character array. and finally transmit the abc value to the pc by using ur. and then in this line this is the definition for abcread function.

here you must start the abc and then wait for conversion to be completed. after that read the abc value from abc data register. and then finally stop the abc and then return the result. this is the result. the potentiometer is connected to pi6. then i will open the serial monitor. here the adc value is printed to the serial monitor. then i will protect the potentiometer. ok for example 2 i will configure the adc in single continuous mode with interrupt mode.

in cube mx you can enable the system debug and then the rcc. after that enable one adc channel for example channel 6. this pin will be connected to a potentiometer as in the previous example. and then enable one gpio for example pb7 as output for led. this led will be used as an indicator so whenever the adc value is larger than result value then this led will be on. after that you can go to configuration tab. here you can configure the adc.

here you can enable the continuous conversion mode. after that go to nfig and then enable the adc global interrupt.

click ok and then after that you can generate the code. here is the main.c file. in this line you can add this code to start the adc in interrupt mode. and then in this line this is the callback function. this function will be called when the adc interrupt is occured. inside this callback function the adc value is compared to 2047. so if the value is larger than 2047 then the yellow led will be on. otherwise it will be off. after that you can build and then download the code. thisis the result. when the potentiometer is in this position the led is off. when i rotate the potentiometer to this position then the led is on.

this condition indicates that the adc value is larger than 2047. ok this is the end of this project. in this project you have learned how to configure adc in polling mode and also in interrupt mode.

ANALOG WATCHDOG AND SCAN MODE

 Hi, welcome to the project number 10.2. In this project, I will teach you how to configure ADC with analog watchdog and then how to configure ADC in scan mode with DMA. So let's get started. After finishing this project, you will be able to configure ADC with analog watchdog and then configure ADC to perform scan compression in DMA mode. Okay this is the example one. In this example, I will show you how to configure analog watchdog to monitor the analog voltage. I will use PA6 for ADC input pin and then set the low threshold value to 1500 and the high threshold value to 2500.

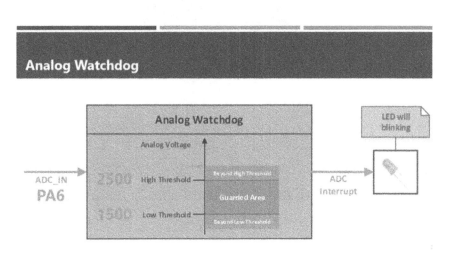

So if the analog voltage is less than 1500 or higher than 2500, then an interrupt will be occur. Inside the interrupt service routine, there are codes for blinking the LED several times. Okay for example one, in cubeMX you can enable the system debug and RCC and then after that enable one ADC channel. For example, I use the channel 6 and then after that you can enable one GPIO pin as output for LED. After that you can go to clock configuration tab. Inside I set the sql frequency to the maximum value which is 72 MHz and then after that go to configuration tab. Here you can configure the ADC one.

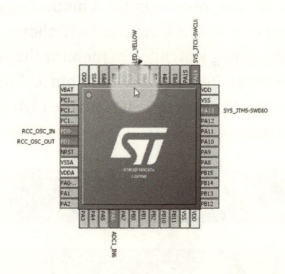

Here you can enable the continuous compression mode and then you can enable the analog watchdog mode. Set the channel to channel 6 and then you can set the high threshold value and also the low threshold value. High threshold value is set to 2500 and low threshold value is set to 1500 and then after that you must enable the interrupt mode.

After that go to end quick settings and then enable the ADC global interrupt. Click ok and then after that you can generate the code. Here is the main.cfile. In this line you can add this code in order to start the ADC in interrupt mode.

 After that in this line the callback function will be called inside the interrupt surface routine when the ADC value is larger than 2500 or lower than 1500.

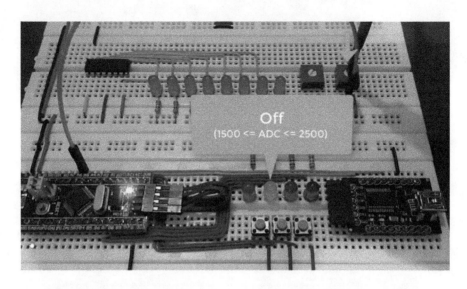

Off
(1500 <= ADC <= 2500)

Inside this function there are codes for blinking the LED several times. After that you can build and then download the code. This is the result. When the potentiometer is in this position the LED is off. Then I will rotate it to this position. As you can see the LED is blinking because the ADC value is less than 1500. Then I will rotate to this position. The LED will off again. When I rotate to this position the LED is blinking again because the ADC value is larger than 28500. Ok this is the example 2. In this example I will configure ADC in scan conversion in order to read 2 ADC channels.

(00:04:15) - The ADC is in continuous mode, so the ADC will do the analog to digital conversion continuously. Then the ADC result will be moved from ADC data register to the ADC value variable by using DMA.

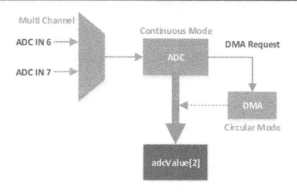

The DMA is in circular mode because the analog to digital conversion run continuously. Ok, for example 2, in cubeMX you can enable the system debug and then the RCC. After that go to ADC, here you can enable two ADC channels, for example channel 6 and then channel 7. And then after that you can enable two GPIO pin as output for LED, yellow LED and green LED. Yellow LED will be used to indicate if the ADC value on channel 6 is higher than a threshold value or not.

If the ADC value is higher than threshold then the LED will be on. The same as yellow LED, the green LED is used for ADC channel 7. After that you can go to configuration tab, here you can configure the ADC one. Here you can change the number of conversion to 2 channels. After that you can set the channel 6 and then channel 7. Here you must change the sampling time to the largest value. After that you can enable the continuous mode and then enable the scan conversion mode. After that you can go to DMA settings. Here you can add DMA channel for ADC, then set the DMA mode to circular mode.

After that click ok and then you can generate the code. Here is the main.g file, here in this line you can add this array for storing the ADC result from channel 6 and 7. After that in this line you can start the ADC in DMA mode.

```
284  /**
285    * @brief  Conversion complete callback in non blocking mode.
286    * @param  hadc: ADC handle
287    * @retval None
288    */
289  void HAL_ADC_ConvCpltCallback(ADC_HandleTypeDef* hadc)
290  {
291    if (adcValue[0] > 2047)
292    {
293      /* Turn yellow LED on */
294      HAL_GPIO_WritePin(LED_YELLOW_GPIO_Port, LED_YELLOW_Pin, GPIO_PIN_SET);
295    }
296    else
297    {
298      /* Turn yellow LED off */
299      HAL_GPIO_WritePin(LED_YELLOW_GPIO_Port, LED_YELLOW_Pin, GPIO_PIN_RESET);
300    }
301
302    if (adcValue[1] > 2047)
303    {
304      /* Turn green LED on */
305      HAL_GPIO_WritePin(LED_GREEN_GPIO_Port, LED_GREEN_Pin, GPIO_PIN_SET);
306    }
307    else
308    {
309      /* Turn green LED off */
310      HAL_GPIO_WritePin(LED_GREEN_GPIO_Port, LED_GREEN_Pin, GPIO_PIN_RESET);
311    }
```

And then this is the callback function that will be called inside the DMA interrupt service routine. The DMA interrupt will be off-channeled whenever the ADC value for each channel has been transferred from ADC data register to ADC value variable. With this function you can compare the ADC value 0 and 1 to 2047. If the ADC value is larger than 2047 then the yellow LED for channel 6 and green LED for channel 7 will be on.

After that you can build and then download the code. This is the result. When I rotate the potentiometer of ADC channel 6 up to this position, then the yellow LED is on. For channel 7 I will rotate the potentiometer up to this position, then the green LED is also on as expected. Ok, this is the end of this project. In this project you have learned how to configure ADC with analog waspdog and then how to configure ADC in scan mode with DMA.

TIMER TRIGGER AND INJECTED CHANNEL

Hi, welcome to the project number 10.3. In this project, I will teach you how to configure ADC with timer trigger and also configure the ADC injected channel. So let's get started. After finishing this project, you will be able to configure ADC with timer trigger so you can set the timer to start the ADC single conversion every 3 seconds. And then after that configure the ADC to perform injected channel conversion. So in order to achieve that, I will show you two examples. This is the example one. In this example, I will configure one timer that will generate trigger signal of ADC conversion every 3 seconds.

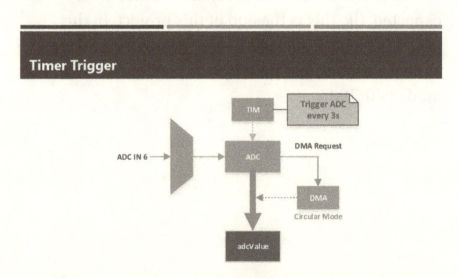

And then the ADC is configured in single shield mode so every trigger ADC will only perform one conversion.

At the end of the conversion, the ADC will generate a DMA request in order to move the ADC value from ADC data register to the ADC value variable. The DMA mode is in circular mode. Okay for example one, in kube-mx you can enable the system debug and rcc as usual. And then after that you can go to ADC, you can enable one channel for example channel 6. And then after that you can enable one timer which is timer 3. In order to know which timer that can be used for ADC trigger, you can look in the reference manual.

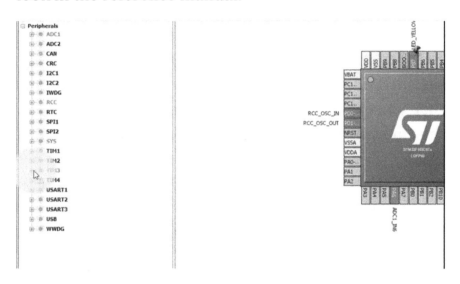

Here in the reference manual, you can see this is the regular channels and these channels can be triggered by the timer. You must choose the timer that has trigger output event which is only the timer 3. So I will choose timer 3 and then enable the internal clock. After that you can enable one GPIO pin as output for LED. This LED will be on if the ADC value is larger than threshold value. And then after that you can go to configuration. Here you can configure the timer 3. Here I set the rescaler to 7200 because my timer clock is 72MHz. So with 7200 I will get 10kHz.

And then after that set the counter period to 30000 so the timer will overflow every 3 seconds. And then enable the update event for the trigger event selection in order for triggering the ADC. Click ok. And then after that you can configure the ADC. Here you can set the external trigger compression soft to timer 3 trigger out event. And then after that you can go to DMA settings. Here you can add one DMA channel for ADC and then set the DMA mode to circular. After that click ok. And then you can generate the code. Here is the my.c file. In this line you can add this variable for storing the ADC value.

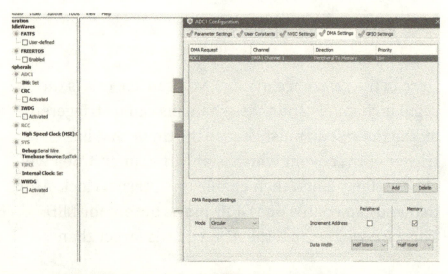

And then in this line you must type the timer3 and also the ADC in DMA mode. In main loop you don't have to add anything. And then here in this line this is the callback function. This function will be called inside the interrupt service routine. Inside this function the ADC value is compared to the threshold value which is 2047. If the ADC value is larger than 2047 then the LED will be on. Otherwise the LED will be off. After that you can build and then download the code. This is the result. The potentiometer is in this position and the LED is off. Then I rotate the potentiometer to this position.

The LED is on but we have to wait up to 3 seconds before the LED is on. This condition happens because the ADC conversion is triggered every 3 seconds by the timer. Ok this is example 2. In this example I will configure 2 ADC channels, channel 6 and channel 7. Channel 6 will be configured as regular channel in continuous mode with DMA.

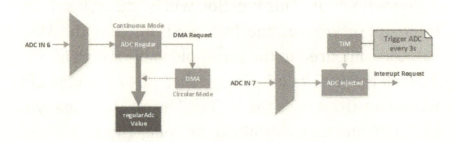

So, the ADC will perform analog to digital contraption on channel 6 continuously and the result will be moved to regular ADC value variable by using DMA. On the other hand, channel 7 will be configured as injected channel with timer trigger every 3 seconds and interrupt mode. So every 3 seconds, ADC will perform a contraption on injected channel which is channel 7 and then after the contraption completed, then the ADC injected interrupt will be generated in order to read the ADC value from ADC injected data register. Ok in cubeMX, you can enable two ADC channels, for example channel 6 and channel 7 and then after that you can enable timer form for triggering the ADC injected channel contraption.

 Here enable the internal clock and then after that enable two GPIO pins as output for LED. These two LED will be on if the ADC values are larger than result value.

The yellow LED is for ADC channel 6 and the green LED is for ADC channel 7. After that go to configuration, configure the timer form, set the tree scalar to 7200 and period to 30000. This is the same settings as in the previous example, so the timer will trigger the ADC conversion every 3 seconds. And also you have to set the trigger event selection to update event and then click ok. After that you can configure the ADC.

Here you can enable the continuous conversion mode for the ADC channel 6 and then set the sampling time of channel 6 to maximum value. After that set one injected channel, set the external trigger soft to timer for trigger of event and then open the settings and change the channel to channel 7. After that go to unfix settings, here you can enable the ADC interrupt for the ADC injected channel and then go to DMA settings. Here you can enable one DMA channel for ADC regular channel and set the DMA mode to circular. After that you can click ok and then you can generate the code.

Here is the main.c file, in this line you can declare the variables for storing the ADC regular and injected channel. In this line you can start the timer for and then start the ADC regular channel in DMA mode and finally you have to start the ADC injected channel in interrupt mode. And then in this line this is the callback function for the ADC regular channel on channel 6. If the value is larger than 2947 then the yellow LED will be on, otherwise the yellow LED will be off. And then in this line this is the callback function for the ADC injected channel.

This function will be called inside the interrupt service routine. Here we must read the ADC value from ADC injected data register and then store in this variable. And then we compare the variable with the threshold value which is 2047. If the value is larger than 2047 then the green LED will be on, otherwise the green LED will be off. Ok after that you can build and then download the code. This is the result. When I rotate the potentiometer on channel 6 to this position, the yellow LED is on. Then back to this position, the yellow LED is off. The same as channel 6, if I rotate the potentiometer to this position, the green LED is on.

But we have to wait up to 3 seconds, because the ADC conversion on this channel is triggered by timer every

3 seconds. Ok this is the end of this project. In this project we have learned how to configure ADC with timer trigger and also configure the ADC to perform uninjected channel conversion.

745595 SHIFT REGISTER

Hi, welcome to the project number 11.1. In this project, I will teach you how to configure SPI peripheral to do a basic data transfer. So let's get started. After finishing this project, you will be able to configure SPI to do a data transfer with the 74595 SIF register IC. Ok, SPI or Serial Peripheral Interface is a synchronous serial communication that used for short-distance communication, usually between components on PCB. SPI bus consists of 4 wires which are CLOCK, MOSI, MISO and SS. The first wire, CLOCK, is used for synchronizing the master device and drive device.

SPI

- Short distance communication.
- Use 4 wires: **CLK, MOSI, MISO, SS**.

The second wire is MOSI, which stands for Master Output Slap Input. This wire will transfer data from master device to slap device. The third wire is MISO, which stands for Master Input Slap Output. This wire will transfer data from slap device to master device. And the last wire is SS, which stands for Slap Select. This wire will activate the slap device. The architecture of SPI bus is master slap that can consist of only one master and more than one slap. In SPI bus, only the master device can initiate a data transfer either from master to slap or slap to master.

Before master can communicate with slap, master must activate the slap by the SS wire.

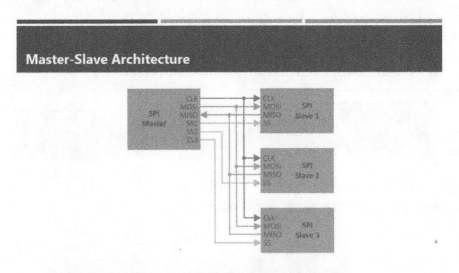

So, only one slap is activated while the other slap is not. This is an illustration for SPI data transfer. Actually SPI data transfer just use slip registers. So within the master device and slap device, there is a slip register.

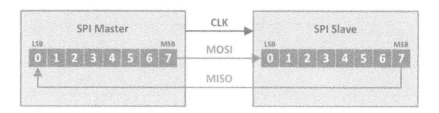

The slip registers are connected by MOSI and MISO line in ring topology. So every one clock, the data bit from master slip register will move to the slap slip register. And after 8 clock, the master and slap have exchanged the register value. This is the SPI data frame.

The data transfer between master and slap device occurs when the SS line is low, because usually the SS pin of the slap devices are active low. There are 8 clock cycles necessary in order to transfer a data byte between master and slap device. The data bit sampling is occurred every rising edge, but it can also be configured every falling edge.

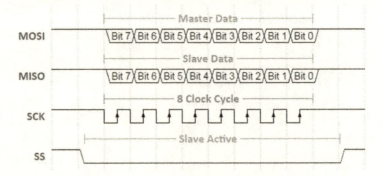

This is the example of the SPI data frame when the master sends character SPI to slap and slap sends character capital B to the master.

Data Frame Example

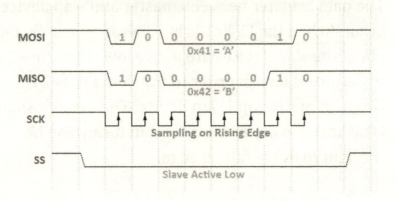

Ok in cubeMX, you can enable the system debug and then the RCC. After that you can enable one SPI peripheral.

- I am using SPI 1. Enable the 4 duplex master mode. This mode will enable 3 GPIO pins which are PA5, 6 and 7 as Cog, Miso and MoSig. I also enable one GPIO pin as output for shift register lights. This pin will be connected to the pin 12 of the 74595 shift register.

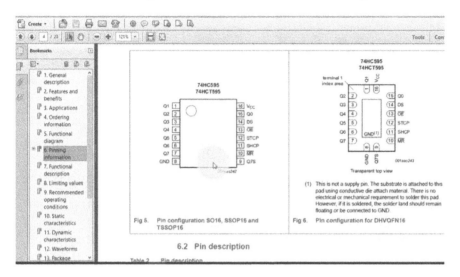

If I look into the datasheet of 74595 shift register, the pin 12 is the storage register clock input. Here in function table, you can see if a rising edge occured on this pin, then the contents of shift register states are transferred to the storage register. The value of storage register will direct the output pins from Q0 to Q6.

Table 3. Function table[1]

Control				Input	Output		Function
SHCP	STCP	OE	MR	DS	Q7S	Qn	
X	X	L	L	X	L	NC	a LOW-level on MR only affects the shift registers
X	↑	L	L	X	L	L	empty shift register loaded into storage register
X	X	H	L	X	L	Z	shift register clear; parallel outputs in high-impedance OFF-state
↑	X	L	H	H	Q6S	NC	logic HIGH-level shifted into shift register stage 0. Contents of all shift register stages shifted through, e.g. previous state of stage 6 (internal Q6S) appears on the serial output (Q7S).
X	↑	L	H	X	NC	QnS	contents of shift register stages (internal QnS) are transferred to the storage register and parallel output stages
↑	↑	L	H	X	Q6S	QnS	contents of shift register shifted through; previous contents of the shift register is transferred to the storage register and the parallel output stages

[1]   H = HIGH voltage state;
L = LOW voltage state;
↑ = LOW-to-HIGH transition;
X = don't care;
NC = no change;
Z = high-impedance OFF-state.

- -

This is Q0 and this is Q6 and these pins will be connected to the LED. And then I also enable one more GPIO pin as input for switch. After that you can go to configuration. You can configure the GPIO.

 For the shift register voltage, I set the GPIO mode to output plus pull and for switch, I enable the pull up resistor. Click ok and then you can configure the HPI one. Here you can change the prescaler in order to set the baud rate. I am using the largest prescaler value which is 256. To do that click ok and then you can generate the code. This is the main.g file. In this line, you can declare these variables for storing the transmit and receive data. Then you can add this function prototype. And this is the definition for this function. The function of this code are basically just generate a rising edge for pin 12 of the shift register.

Then in main program, there are three functions that can be used for HPI data transfer. The first function is how HPI transmit. This function will transmit data bytes in polling mode. And then the second function is how HPI receive. This function will receive data bytes in polling mode. And then the third function is how HPI transmit receive. This function will transmit and receive data at the same time in polling mode. First before transmit or receive the data, the program will wait for the user button press. Then after that if the button is pressed, then we transmit 0 to the shift register.

Then let the shift register in order to transfer the value from the shift register to the output buffer register. So the LED will be on or off depending on the value inside this register. Then you must add this delay to avoid button debouncing. In these codes, we only transmit data bytes to shift register, but we not read data bytes from shift register. On the other hand, in these codes, we will transmit 1 to the shift register and receive 0 from shift register, because previously we transmit 0 to the shift register. And then, in this line we transmit 2 to the shift register and receive 1 from shift register, because previously we transmit 1 to the shift register.

And then in this line, we transmit 3 to the shift register and receive 2 from the shift register, because previously we transmit 2 in this line. Finally, we only reset data which is 3 from the Z-Predecessor. After that, you can build and then download the code. This is the result. I run the program in debug mode and I will monitor the value of rxdata variable. I press the switch. Here as you can see, all of the LED are turned off which are equal to 0 because we send 0 in this line. Then I press the switch again. The LED are equal to 1 and the content of rxdata variable is 0.

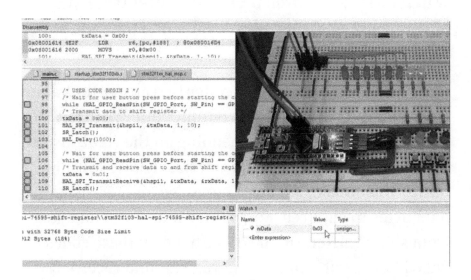

Then I press the switch again. Here as you can see, the LED are equal to 2 and the content of rxdata variable is updated to 1. Then I press the switch again. The LED are equal to 3 and the content of rxdata variable is updated to 2. And finally, I press the switch again. The LED are still 3 because we only reset data from Z-Predecessor and the content of rxdata variable is updated to 3. So that is how the SPI bus works. Okay this is the end of this project. In this project you have learned how to configure SPI to communicate with 74595 Z-Predecessor IC.

LIS302DL ACCELEROMETER

Hi, welcome to the project number 11.2. In this project, I will teach you how to configure SPI territorial to communicate with LIS302DL as a lower method.

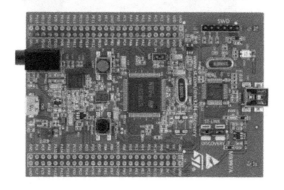

LIS302DL Accelerometer

So please start it. After finishing this project, you will be able to configure SPI to communicate with LIS302DL as a lower method. Okay in this project, I will use the STM32F4 Discovery Board. There is already a built-in LIS302DL as a lower method on this board. If you don't have the STM32F4 Discovery Board, then you can use a standalone LIS302DL module. Okay in

CubeMX, you can create a project for STM32F407 VGT because the STM32F4 Discovery use this chip.

Then you can enable the system debug and then also enable the SPI in full duplex master mode. And also you have to enable one GPIO as output for SSLINE which is PE3.

This GPIO is connected to the SS pin of the accelerometer. For the system clock, I use the default setting which is 16 MHz. Then after that go to configuration. You have to configure the GPIO. And then change the GPIO output level to HIGH. Then after that you can configure the SPI one. Then change the pitch color to FADE. Now the VALUE is 2 Mbps. After that click OK. And then you can generate the code.

Okay here is the MINDLUCY file. Here in this slide you can add these three variables for storing the register address, transmit data and Y-axis accelerometer data. And then here in main program you can add these codes. The function of these codes is to enable the accelerometer Y-axis.

7.2 CTRL_REG1 (20h)

Table 18. CTRL_REG1 (20h) register

DR	PD	FS	STP	STM	Zen	Yen	Xen

Table 19. CTRL_REG1 (20h) register description

DR	Data rate selection. Default value: 0 (0: 100 Hz output data rate; 1: 400 Hz output data rate)
PD	Power Down Control. Default value: 0 (0: power down mode; 1: active mode)
FS	Full Scale selection. Default value: 0 (refer to Table 3 for typical full scale value)
STP, STM	Self Test Enable. Default value: 0 (0: normal mode; 1: self test P, M enabled)
Zen	Z axis enable. Default value: 1 (0: Z axis disabled; 1: Z axis enabled)
Yen	Y axis enable. Default value: 1 (0: Y axis disabled; 1: Y axis enabled)
Xen	X axis enable. Default value: 1 (0: X axis disabled; 1: X axis enabled)

According to the data sheet of the accelerometer, to enable the accelerometer we have to configure the control register one. We must set this bit to power up the accelerometer. And then set this bit to 1 to enable the Y-axis. These two bits are correspond to 42 in hexadecimal.

And in order to write a value to this register through SPI communication, we must send the address of this register which is 20 followed by the register value which is 42. Here in this line we send the register address which is 20. And then in this line we send the data which is 42 through the SPI by using HAL SPI transmit function. Before we can communicate to the accelerometer, we must enable the accelerometer by writing low to the SS pin. And then after the transmission is completed, we can disable the accelerometer by writing high to the SS pin. And then in main loop we can write codes for reading the Y-axis data.

First we have to set the SS pin to low to enable the accelerometer. And then we must send the register address that we are trying to read from which is 29 in hexadecimal. This is the register address for Y-axis data. Then we must add 80 in hexadecimal to this address in order to tell the accelerometer that we are trying to read data from it. Then this code will receive the Y-axis data and store the data in this variable. And finally we have to disable the accelerometer. Okay after that we can build and then download the code. This is the result. I run the code in debug mode and monitor the Y-axis data.

As you can see this is the Y-axis data. Then I rotate the STM32 to the positive angle direction. Here as you can see the value is implicit. And then I rotate it to the negative angle direction.

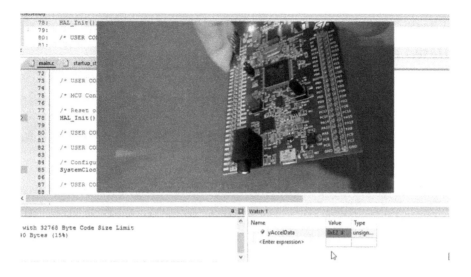

Here you can see the value is decreasing. Okay this is the end of this project. In this project we have learned how to configure SPI to communicate with LIS302DL accelerometer.

AT24C08 EEPROM

Hi, welcome to the project number 12.1. In this project, I will teach you how to configure I2C communication. So, let's get started. After finishing this project, you will be able to configure I2C in BMA mode to communicate with AT24C08DE from IC. Inter-integrated circuit, or often pronounced as I2C or I2C, is a synchronous serial communication. This protocol was developed by Pilip Semiconductor and is used to interact between different ICs on motherboard. The I2C bus needs two wires to make a communication between two devices, and because of that, some products sometimes referred as two-wire interface or TWI.

These two wires are Serial Clock Line or SCL and Serial Data Line or SDA.

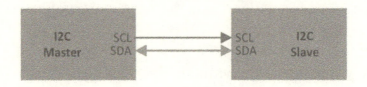

- Short distance communication.
- Use 2 wires (**Two Wire Interface** or **TWI**): **SCL**, **SDA**.

Serial Clock Line is the Serial Clock and the Serial Data Line is a bidirectional data line used for transmit and receive data. Because I2C only use one data line, then the communication mode is half duplex. So, the transmitting or receiving process can occur on the same data line, but not at the same time. Just like SPI, I2C is a master bus, but has several differences.

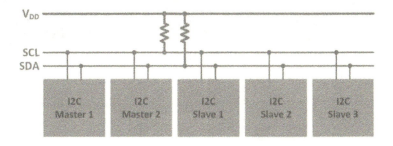

The first difference with SPI is that in I2C, we can have more than one master device, therefore we called multi-master multi-slot.

The second difference with SPI is that the SCL and SDA pin on I2C are open drain pins, so we need pull-up resistors to pull the SCL and SDA line to VDD. This is the I2C protocol. This protocol is for writing data from master to slave. Prior to any transaction on the I2C bus, master must send a stop condition to all slave devices. Also, when the data transfer is finished, then master must send a stop condition to inform other devices that it would like to release the bus. Here, after stop condition, master will send the slave address followed by read or write bit to the I2C bus.

In this case, we set the read or write bit to 0 because we want to write data to slave. If we want to read data from slave, then we must set this bit to 1. When a slave has been addressed, then the slave will generate an acknowledge.

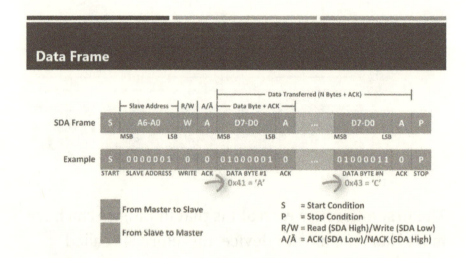

And also, when every data has been received, the slave will generate an acknowledge. Slave can generate acknowledge signal by pulling the SDA line to low. After the slave has been addressed and acknowledge signal from slave is received by master, then master can send data bytes to the slave. In this example, master sends capital A and capital C to the slave.

Ok, this is the data frame for reading data from slave.

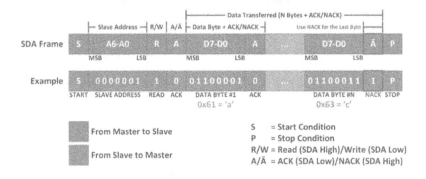

Read operation is initiated in the same way as write operation as in previous slide. The difference is that the read to write byte is set to 1. Then after the slave responds with acknowledge signal, slave will send the data byte to master, followed by acknowledge signal from master every data byte that has been received by master. If the transmitted data is the final byte, then master will not generate an acknowledge signal, but will generate a stop condition. In this example, master with data A and C from the slave.

This is the start and stop condition. The start condition is generated by master by pulling the SDA line to low followed by SCA line.

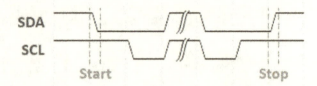

And the stop condition is also generated by master by releasing the SCA line followed by SDA line. Ok, in this demo, I will demonstrate I2C communication with IT24C or A from IC. In cubeMX, you can enable the system debug and then the FCC. After that, you can enable one I2C peripheral. I am using I2C2. Here you can enable the I2C mode.

This I2C peripheral will enable two pins as SDA and SCL. And also after that you have to enable one GPIO pin as output for LED which is PB8 and as input for switch which is PC15.

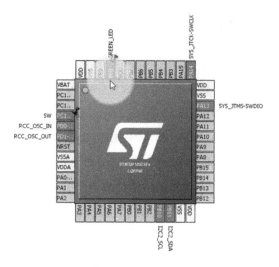

Then after that you can go to configuration. Here you can configure the GPIO for the LED. I set the GPIO mode to output push pull and for the switch I set the pull up resistor. Click ok and then after that you can configure the I2C. For the I2C I will use the default settings. After that you can go to DMA settings.

Here you can add two DMA channels for I2C transmit and I2C receive.

And then after that you can click ok and then you can generate the code. Here is the main.g file. Here in this line this is the definition for euprom device address. According to the data sheet of this euprom which is 8 kilo euprom, the first 4 bits of the device address is A in hexadecimal and the bit 3 corresponds to the pin A2 of the euprom. In this case I connect the pin A2 of the euprom to ground so the bit 3 of the device address is 0. Therefore we define the device address as A0 in hex. The bit 2 and bit 1 are not used for 8 kilo euprom and you must set this bit to 0 because these 2 bits will be used for page address.

The bit 0 corresponds to the right bit and this bit will be set of clip inside the half function.

increment the data word address and serially clock out sequential data words. When the memory address limit is reached, the data word address will "roll over" and the sequential read will continue. The sequential read operation is terminated when the microcontroller does not respond with a zero but does generate a following stop condition (see Figure 12 on page 11).

Figure 7. Device Address

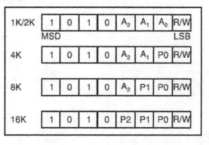

Then after that you have to declare the text that will be stored inside the euprom. Then after that I write 3 functions that can be used for writing and reading data to and from the euprom and also a function for comparing the contents of two buffers. And then in main function the program will wait until the switch is pressed. Then write the text that we have defined to the euprom page 0. Then after that we must wait until the euprom is ready for any operation.

Then we read the euprom page 0 to check if the data that has been written to the page 0 of the euprom is correct or not. And then here in this line this is the definition for euprom write function. Here in this line you must define the device address followed by page address in this format. This is the device address and the page address and this is the rest of the euprom page address. After that in this line you can use how I2C memory write DMA function in order to write data to euprom with I2C in DMA mode. And then this is the definition for I2C read data function.

The procedure is the same as when we write data to euprom. This is the address definition that's exactly the same as in previous function. But in this line instead of write we use read function to read data from euprom. And finally this is the definition for buffer compare function. This is the callback function for DMA receive. So after the data is read by I2C and transferred by DMA to euprom data variable then this callback function will be called in order to compare the data that has been written to euprom with the original data. If the data is the same as the original then the green LED will be on.

Ok after that you can build and then download the code. This is the result.

I will refresh the switch. Here as you can see the green LED is on which indicates that the data that has been written to euprom is the same as the original data. So the program works as expected. Ok this is the end of this project. In this project you have learned how to configure I2C to communicate with AT24C08EUPROMIC.

TWO-BOARDS COMMUNICATION

Hi, welcome to the project number 12.2. In this project, I will teach you how to configure two STM32 boards as

I2C slave and I2C master, so the master board can communicate with the slave board. So let's get started. After finishing this project, you will be able to configure STM32 boards as a simple I2C slave device and also configure another STM32 board as I2C master to communicate with the I2C slave board. So you need two STM32 boards for this project. Okay this is the block diagram of the system that we will create in this project. This is the I2C slave device and I use the STM32F103 and then this is the I2C master device, I use the STM32F4 discovery board.

 In slave device, I will configure one GPIO as output for LED and then I will control this LED from the master device.

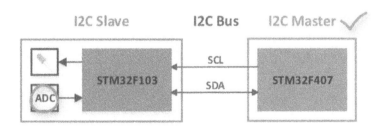

And I also configure one ADC channel in slave device, then I will read the ADC value from master device through the I2C bus. Now I will configure the

STM32F103 as I2C slave. In QPemx, you can enable the system debug and then the RCC.

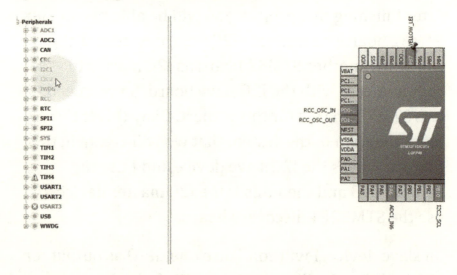

After that you can enable one I2C peripheral, for example I2C2, enable the I2C mode and then after that you can enable one GPIO as output for LED, for example PB7. And then after that you can enable one ADC channel, for example channel 6.

And then after that you can go to configuration. Of the ADC, I will use the default settings. Then you can configure the I2C.

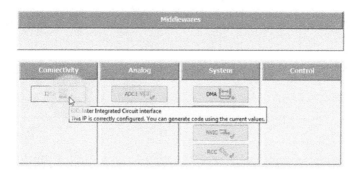

For I2C, here I set the slave address to 4 in hexadecimal, this address is in 7 bit format. After that click ok. And then you can generate the code. This is the main.c file. Before I explain the main code, I will show you something in I2C init function. Here is the I2C init function. This function is generated by QPemx. As you can see here, the slave address is set to 8, but previously we set the slave address in QPemx to 4. Here the slave address is 4.

But in this code the slave address is 8. This is happen because the QPemx converts the 7 bit address to 8 bit left aligned address. Because the bit 0 is for the right bit of the I2C dataframe. Ok now let's go to the main program.

```
main.c
248    sConfig.SamplingTime = ADC_SAMPLETIME_1CYCLE_5;
249    if (HAL_ADC_ConfigChannel(&hadc1, &sConfig) !=
250    {
251      _Error_Handler(__FILE__, __LINE__);
252    }
253
254    }
255
256    /* I2C2 init function */
257    static void MX_I2C2_Init(void)
258    {
259
260      hi2c2.Instance = I2C2;
261      hi2c2.Init.ClockSpeed = 100000;
262      hi2c2.Init.DutyCycle = I2C_DUTYCYCLE_2;
263      hi2c2.Init.OwnAddress1 = 8;
264      hi2c2.Init.AddressingMode = I2C_ADDRESSINGMODE_7BIT;
265      hi2c2.Init.DualAddressMode = I2C_DUALADDRESS_DISABLE;
266      hi2c2.Init.OwnAddress2 = 0;
267      hi2c2.Init.GeneralCallMode = I2C_GENERALCALL_DISABLE;
268      hi2c2.Init.NoStretchMode = I2C_NOSTRETCH_DISABLE;
269      if (HAL_I2C_Init(&hi2c2) != HAL_OK)
270      {
271        _Error_Handler(__FILE__, __LINE__);
272      }
273
274    }
275
```

	MSB							LSB	
	0	0	0	0	1	0	0		= 0x4

7-bit Address

	MSB							LSB	
	0	0	0	1	0	0	0		= 0x8

7-bit Address (Left Aligned) R/W

Here in main program, the slave address always wait for a transfer request from master. The request from master can be vitalid or readidc.

```
116    while (HAL_I2C_Slave_Receive(&hi2c2, (uint8_t*)&transferRequest, 1, 10) != HAL_OK);
117    /* Wait until I2C is ready */
118    while (HAL_I2C_GetState(&hi2c2) != HAL_I2C_STATE_READY);
119
120    /* If master request write LED operation */
121    if (transferRequest == MASTER_REQ_WRITE_LED)
122    {
123      /* Slave receives data from master */
124      while (HAL_I2C_Slave_Receive(&hi2c2, (uint8_t*)&ledValue, 1, 10) != HAL_OK);
125      /* Wait until I2C is ready */
126      while (HAL_I2C_GetState(&hi2c2) != HAL_I2C_STATE_READY);
127
128      /* Turn on or off the LED depending on the command from master */
129      if (ledValue)
130      {
131        HAL_GPIO_WritePin(YELLOW_LED_GPIO_Port, YELLOW_LED_Pin, GPIO_PIN_SET);
132      }
133      else
134      {
135        HAL_GPIO_WritePin(YELLOW_LED_GPIO_Port, YELLOW_LED_Pin, GPIO_PIN_RESET);
136      }
137    }
138    /* If master request read ADC operation */
139    else if (transferRequest == MASTER_REQ_READ_ADC)
140    {
141      uint8_t tmpAdcValue[2];
142
```

If master request to write LED, then these codes will be executed. This line will receive the LED value from

164

master either on or off. And then this line will turn on or off the LED depending on the LED value that received from master. If master request to read ADC, then these codes will be executed. This line will start the ADC and then wait for ADC confession to be completed. And then after that, read the ADC value from ADC data register and finally stop the ADC. And then after that, before we send this ADC value to master, we must split the ADC height and low value because the ADC value is 12 bits and the I2C can only send 8 bit data.

```
140    {
141        uint8_t tmpAdcValue[2];
142
143        /* Enable ADC and start ADC conversion */
144        HAL_ADC_Start(&hadc1);
145        /* Wait for ADC conversion to be completed */
146        HAL_ADC_PollForConversion(&hadc1, 1);
147        /* Get ADC value from ADC data register */
148        adcValue = HAL_ADC_GetValue(&hadc1);
149        /* Stop ADC conversion and disable ADC */
150        HAL_ADC_Stop(&hadc1);
151
152        /* Split the ADC high and low value */
153        /* Get ADC value from bit 0 to 7 */
154        tmpAdcValue[0] = adcValue & 0xFF;
155        /* Get ADC value from bit 8 to 11 */
156        tmpAdcValue[1] = adcValue >> 8;
157
158        /* Slave transmit ADC value to master */
159        while (HAL_I2C_Slave_Transmit(&hi2c2, (uint8_t*)tmpAdcValue, 2, 10) != HAL_OK);
160        /* Wait until I2C is ready */
161        while (HAL_I2C_GetState(&hi2c2) != HAL_I2C_STATE_READY);
162    }
163    }
164    /* USER CODE END 3 */
165
166 }
167
```

The ADC value from bit 0 to 7 is stored in element 0 of this array and ADC value from bit 8 to 11 is stored in element 1. After that, you can transmit this array to the master device. Ok after that, you can build and then download the code. Ok now I will configure the

165

STM32F for discovery as I2C master. In cubeMX you can enable the system debug and then after that you can enable the I2C peripera. Then after that go to configuration. For I2C configuration, I will use the default settings and then you can click ok and generate the code. Ok this is the main.c file for master device.

Here in this line I define the slave address which is 8 in hexadecimal in 8 bit left aligned format. And then define the master request for write LED and read ADC. In main loop, every 1 second I will configure master to request write LED and read ADC to slave. First we must transmit the request to the slave followed by LED value. The LED value is toggled every 1 second. Then for reading the ADC value, first we transmit the request to the slave. Then the I2C slave will send the ADC high and low value. After that we must combine the ADC high and low value and store the result in this variable.

Ok after that you can breathe and then download the code. This is the result. As you can see the LED is blinking every 1 second. And I also run the master device in debug mode so you can see the ADC value. The ADC channel 6 is connected to the potentiometer. I rotate the potentiometer. Here you can see the ADC value is updated.

Ok this is the end of this project. In this project we have learned how to configure two STM32 box as I2C slave and I2C master so the master can communicate with the slave.

WINDOW WACHDOG, INDEPENDENT WATCHDOG

Hi, welcome to the project number 13. In this project, I will teach you how to configure Window WasDoc Timer and Independent WasDoc Timer. So, let's get started. After finishing this project, you will be able to configure the Window WasDoc Timer and also the Independent WasDoc Timer in order to reset the STM32. A WasDoc Timer is a timer that can be used to detect software anomalies and reset the processor if any occurs.

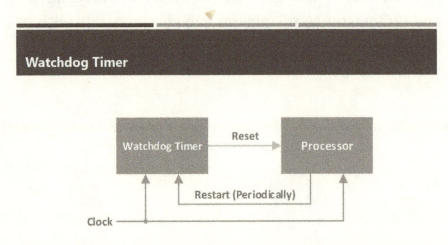

A WasDoc Timer is necessary for designing a reliable embedded system because it is not usually possible to wait for someone to reboot the processor if the software hangs.

A WasDoc Timer is just a counter that codes down from initial value to zero. The software must periodically restart the counter value to the initial value before it reaches zero. If the counter reaches zero before the software restarts it, then the software is presumed to be hanged. Then the WasDoc will reset the processor. In STM32, there are two types of WasDoc Timer, Window WasDoc and Independent WasDoc. In Window WasDoc, there is a limited window between window value and timer value. So the counter value must be reset within the window. If not, then the STM32 will be reset by the Window WasDoc.

On the other hand, the Independent WasDoc of STM32 is just a regular WasDoc Timer.

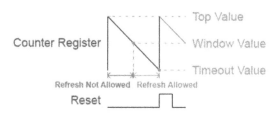

Window Watchdog Timer

There is no window where the value must be reset, the difference with Window WasDoc is that the Independent WasDoc is clocked by its own dedicated low-speed internal clock and it will stay active even if the main clock fails. Okay, in this demo, I will show you two examples. In example 1, I will configure the Window WasDoc and in example 2, I will configure the Independent WasDoc. Now for example 1, I enable the System Debug and then the RCC.

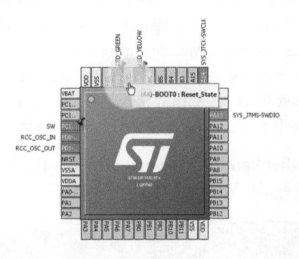

After that, I enable the Window WasDoc and I also enable 2 GPIO pins as output or LED.

And I also enable one GPIO pin as input or switch. After that, go to clock configuration, I set the 6 clock frequency to 72 MHz and then go to configuration. Here you can configure the Window WasDoc.

Figure 183. Watchdog block diagram

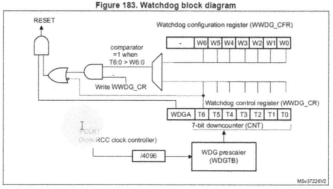

The application program must write in the WWDG_CR register at regular intervals during normal operation to prevent an MCU reset. This operation must occur only when the counter value is lower than the window register value. The value to be stored in the WWDG_CR

According to the reference manual of STM32, the Window WasDoc is clocked from P-Clock 1. The value of P-Clock 1 is 36 MHz. The P-Clock 1 will be divided by 4096 and also will be divided again by WasDoc Prescaler. In configuration, I set the WasDoc Prescaler to 8. So the WasDoc Timer Frequency is 36 MHz divided by 4096 and divided again by 8. So the frequency is 1099 Hz.

The Window WasDoc has 7 bit down counter register, so the maximum initial value is 127. I set the counter value to the maximum and then here you can set the window value which is 80. With this top value and window value, you can calculate the window duration which is from 43 ms and 58 ms. So you can refresh the Window WasDoc within this duration between 43 ms and 58 ms. Otherwise the WasDoc reset will be occured. After that click ok and then you can generate

171

the code. Ok this is the myndotc file. Here in this line you must enable the Window WasDoc and then after that in this line I check the WasDoc reset flag so if the system has been reset by the Window WasDoc then the yellow LED will be on.

Otherwise the green LED will be on. In my loop I add 50 ms delay. In real application you should replace this delay with your application code.

```
109     HAL_GPIO_WritePin(LED_GREEN_GPIO_Port, LED_GREEN_Pin, GPIO_PIN_SET);
110   }
111     /* USER CODE END 2 */
112
113     /* Infinite loop */
114     /* USER CODE BEGIN WHILE */
115     while (1)
116     {
117     /* USER CODE END WHILE */
118
119     /* USER CODE BEGIN 3 */
120       /* WWDG clock = (PCLK1(36MHz)/4096)/8) = 1099 Hz (~910 us)
121        * Timeout = ~910 us * (127-63) = 58 ms
122        * Refresh = ~910 us * (127-80) = 43 ms
123        * Window = 43 ms to 58 ms */
124       HAL_Delay(50);
125
126       while (HAL_GPIO_ReadPin(SW_GPIO_Port, SW_Pin) == GPIO_PIN_RESET);
127
128       HAL_WWDG_Refresh(&hwwdg, 127);
129   }
130     /* USER CODE END 3 */
131
132   }
133
134  /** System Clock Configuration
135  */
136  void SystemClock_Config(void)
```

But the duration of your application must be within 43 ms to 58 ms because the Window WasDoc is allowed to be reset within this period.

And then this code is for restart the content value. And I also add code for simulating the software hang by this loop. So if the switch is pressed, then the CPU will execute this loop until the switch is released. Therefore, the window wasdog is not refreshed within the window, then the wasdog reset will be occurred. Ok, after that, you can build and then download the code. This is the result. After you download the code, the yellow LED may be already turned on. So first you can reset the STM32. Then the green LED is on, which is indicated that the window wasdog reset is not occurred.

Then if I press the switch, then the window wasdog will be occurred. Here you can see after I press the switch, the window wasdog is occurred. Then reset the STM32, so the yellow LED is on. Now I will change the delay to 42 milliseconds. And then, rebuild the code and download the code again. This is the result when I press the reset button. The yellow LED is still on because the delay is 42, so the window wasdog time up is refreshed outside the window value. So the window wasdog reset is always occurred. Ok, now I will show you example 2. In this example, I will configure the independent wasdog timer.

First in cubeMX, you can enable the system debug and then the RCC. After that, you can enable the independent wasdog. And I also enable 2 GPIO pins as output for LED. And also 1 GPIO pin as input for switch. After that, go to clock configuration. Here I set the sysclock frequency to 72 MHz. And then here you can also know the clock frequency for independent wasdog timer which is 40 kHz. Then go to configuration. Here you can configure the independent wasdog. I set the prescalar to 32. So the independent wasdog clock will be 40 kHz divided by 32 which is 1.25 kHz.

Then I set the wasdog counter reload value to 4095. This is the maximum value for the reload value. So the independent wasdog timeout will be occurred after about 3.2 seconds. So we must refresh the independent wasdog counter within this period. After that, you can click ok. And then you can generate the code.

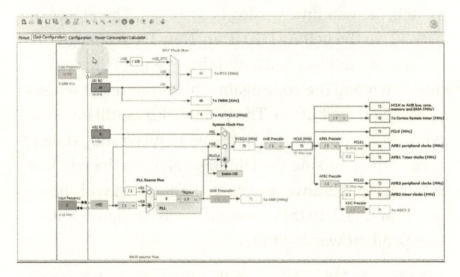

Ok, this is the mine.c file. Here in this line, you must start the independent wasdog timer. And then I also read the independent wasdog reset flag. So if the system has been reset by independent wasdog, the yellow LED will be on. Otherwise the green LED will be on.

In mine loop, here is the function for refreshing the independent wasdog counter value. And I also add this line in order to simulate the software hang because if I press the switch, then the execution of the code will be stuck in this while loop. Therefore the refresh function is not executed and after timeout, the independent wasdog will reset the STM32. Ok after that, you can build and then download the code. This is the result. The green LED is on, indicated that the independent wasdog reset is not occurred.

When I press the switch, more than 3 seconds, then the yellow LED is on because the independent wasdog reset is occurred.

Ok this is the end of this project. In this project we have learned how to configure the window wasdog timer and independent wasdog timer.

SLEEP MODE, STOP MODE, AND STANDBY MODE

Hi, welcome to the project number 14. In this project, I will teach you how to configure the STM32 in low power modes. So let's get started.

After finishing this project, you will be able to configure the STM32 in low power modes. The STM32 F1 has 3 low power modes which are sleep mode, stop mode, and standby mode.

Low-Power Modes

Mode name	Entry	wakeup	Effect on 1.8V domain clocks	Effect on V_{DD} domain clocks	Voltage regulator
Sleep (Sleep now or Sleep-on-exit)	WFI	Any interrupt	CPU clock OFF no effect on other clocks or analog clock sources	None	ON
	WFE	Wakeup event			
Stop	PDDS and LPDS bits + SLEEPDEEP bit + WFI or WFE	Any EXTI line (configured in the EXTI registers)	All 1.8V domain clocks OFF	HSI and HSE oscillators OFF	ON or in low-power mode (depends on Power control register (PWR_CR))
Standby	PDDS bit + SLEEPDEEP bit + WFI or WFE	WKUP pin rising edge, RTC alarm, external reset in NRST pin, IWDG reset			OFF

This table summarizes the effects of low power modes to the clocks and voltage regulator and also describes how to wake up the STM32 from low power modes. For sleep mode, you can wake up the STM32 from sleep mode by an interrupt or wake up event depending on the entry mode. The main difference between interrupt

176

and event is that if interrupt occurs, then the interrupt service routine will be executed.

But if event occurs, then there is no interrupt service routine will be executed. In sleep mode, only the CPU clock is off while another clock and the voltage regulator is still on.

And then for stop mode, you can wake up the STM32 by using any external interrupt. In stop mode, all the 1.8 domain clock and the high speed internal and external clock is turned off while the voltage regulator can be on or in low power mode depending on the configuration.

For the standby mode, in order to wake up the STM32, you can use either the wake up pin, FTC alarm, external reset pin, or the independent watchdog reset. In standby mode, all the 1.8 domain clock and the high speed internal and external clock is turned off and also the voltage regulator is turned off. Each low power mode has different power consumption. The lowest power consumption is achieved when the STM32 is configured in standby mode. Ok, in this demo, i will show you 3 examples in order to configure the STM32 in sleep mode, stop mode, and standby mode.

For the first example, i will configure the STM32 in sleep mode. In QPMX, you have to enable the system debug and then the FCC.

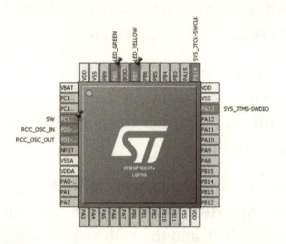

After that, you can enable 2 GPIO pins as output for LED and 1 GPIO pin as input for switch.

And then go to configuration, you can configure the GPIO, set the pull up resistor for switch and set the GPIO mode to external interrupt with calling as trigger detection. Because i will use this switch to generate external interrupt in order to wake up the STM32 from the sleep mode. Ok, after that, click ok and then you can generate the code. This is the main.c file. Here in this line, i write a function prototype called power enter sleep mode. So when this function is called, then the STM32 will enter the sleep mode.

```
  87    /* USER CODE END SysInit */
  88
  89    /* Initialize all configured peripherals */
  90    MX_GPIO_Init();
  91
  92    /* USER CODE BEGIN 2 */
  93    PWR_EnterSleepMode();
  94    /* USER CODE END 2 */
  95
  96    /* Infinite loop */
  97    /* USER CODE BEGIN WHILE */
  98    while (1)
  99    {
 100      /* USER CODE END WHILE */
 101
 102      /* USER CODE BEGIN 3 */
 103        HAL_GPIO_TogglePin(LED_YELLOW_GPIO_Port, LED_YELLOW_Pin);
 104        HAL_Delay(1000);
 105      }
 106      /* USER CODE END 3 */
 107
 108    }
 109
 110  /** System Clock Configuration
 111  */
 112  void SystemClock_Config(void)
 113  {
 114
```

This function is called here, so after initialization
process, then the STM32 will enter the sleep mode.

Therefore, this code inside main loop is not executed.
This code is executed only after the STM32 is wake up
from sleep mode. And then here, this is the definition
for enter sleep mode function. Inside this function, the
sysstick timer is suspended because if not, then the
sysstick interrupt will wake up the STM32 from sleep
mode. And in this line, you can enter the sleep mode. So
the codes below this line will be executed only after the
STM32 is wake up from sleep mode. And after wake
up, the sysstick timer is resumed. And then here in this
line, this is the callback function for the external
interrupt. So if this switch is pressed, then the green
LED will be on. Okay, after that you can build and then
download the code. This is the result. Now the STM32
is in sleep mode, therefore the yellow LED is not

blinking. Then I press the switch. The green LED is on and the yellow LED is blinking because the STM32 has been wake up from sleep mode.

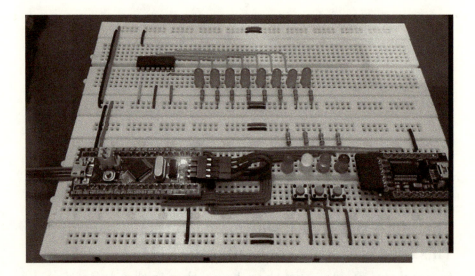

When your STM32 is in sleep mode, you cannot download the program to the STM32.

- You will get this message. So, in order to download the program, you must press and hold the reset button, and then press the download button, and release the reset button. Okay for example 2, I will configure the stop mode. The procedure is similar to sleep mode. In cubeMX you can enable the system debug and then the RCC. After that you can enable one GPIO pin as output for LED, and one GPIO pin as input for switch. And then go to configuration, configure the GPIO. For input pin, I set the GPIO mode to external event mode with falling edge trigger detection, and I also set the pullout resistor.

This switch will be used to wake up the STM32 from stop mode, but instead of external interrupt, in this example I will use the external event. And then you can click ok, and generate the code. This is the mind.c file. In this line, this is the function prototype for entering the stop mode. Same in this line, after initialization process, the STM32 will enter the stop mode, and then in main loop, this code will be executed only after the STM32 is wake up from stop mode. Then this is the definition for enter stop mode function. First you have to suspend the CTK timer, then enter the stop mode.

So the code below this line will be executed only after the STM32 is wake up from stop mode. After wake up, the sysclock config function is called again in this line, because when entering stop mode, the highspeed external and highspeed internal oscillator is turned off, and the default clock selected after wake up is the highspeed internal. So this function will set the system clock back to highspeed external clock again. And then after that you can resume the CTK timer. Ok as you can see here, there is no callback function like in the previous example, because in this example I use the external event instead of external interrupt.

Ok after that you can build and then download the code. This is the result, now the STM32 is in stop mode, therefore the yellow LED is not blinking, then I press the switch, the yellow LED is blinking because the STM32 has been wake up from stop mode. Ok now for example 3, I will configure the standby mode. In cubeMX you can enable the system debug and then the RCC, and I also enable the independent watchdog, because in this example I will use the independent watchdog in order to wake up the STM32 from standby mode. Then I also enable one GPIO pin as output for LED.

After that go to configuration, here you can configure the independent watchdog. I set the prescaler to 64 and the counter value to 4095, so the independent watchdog timeout value is about 6.5 seconds. After that click ok and then you can generate the code. This is the main.c file, here in this line I start the independent watchdog and then in main loop I blink the yellow LED for several times. After that I put the STM32 in standby mode by this function. Here as you can see in main loop there is no code for refreshing the independent watchdog timer, therefore the independent watchdog timer always occur every 6.5 seconds. Then will reset the STM32. This reset will wake up the STM32 from standby mode. Ok after that you can build and then download the code. This is the result. Here as you can see the yellow LED is blinking several times. Then the STM32 will enter standby mode and after the independent watchdog timer is occurred then the independent watchdog reset is occurred to wake up the STM32 from standby mode, therefore the yellow LED is blinking again. Ok this is the end of this project.

In this project we have learned how to configure the STM32 in low power modes.